VISUAL

SELLING

CAPTURE THE EYE AND

THE CUSTOMER WILL FOLLOW

PAUL LEROUX AND PEG CORWIN

BICENTENNIAL
1807
WILEY
2007
BICENTENNIAL

John Wiley & Sons, Inc.

165101

To John Noonan, PhD, vice president of organizational development and training for Conseco, Inc. For the past 17 years, John has shown tremendous support and faith in my work, and has provided the avenue for bringing me, and the messages in this book, into multiple corporations.

And to Mark Chandler, PhD, Ralph McDade, PhD, and Mike Spain, MD, the founders of Rules-Based Medicine, Luminex, and Biophysical Corporations. Mark, Ralph, and Mike swear by images and understand visual selling better than anybody I have ever met.

Contents

CONTENTS

Part III
Selling Situations

Preface

Before PowerPoint, sellers worked hard to create a persuasive pitch. They won or lost by how well they held and guided the prospects' attention. Unfortunately, PowerPoint changed this scenario. The center of attention is now the screen or even worse, a handout. Sellers have become projectionists, throwing words on a screen while listeners read ahead and sellers plod behind, mouthing what's already been displayed. PowerPoint's electronic barrage of words, bullet points, and sentences threaten to turn the art of persuasion into a lost art.

It's likely all this is familiar to you. You have fallen into the PowerPoint routine and your ability to sell has been hurt as a result. You probably have lost sales because your ability to persuade has taken a back seat to your ability to "project."

The good news is that it doesn't have to be this way. By being aware of all the visual tools at your disposal and using them effectively, you can return the prospects' attention to where it belongs—on you. More importantly, you can use these visual tools to increase the persuasive power of your pitch.

This book is written to help you achieve these goals.

Crippling the Seller

PowerPoint can be a powerful tool, but when used incorrectly it undermines sellers in two ways:

1. The screen commands center stage because it displays the message.
2. Prospects read text rather than pay attention to the seller.

Consider how PowerPoint presentations cripple even the best salespeople as the selling process evolves. In high-dollar, competitive situations, many proposals are submitted. A weeding process narrows the contenders to a few who are chosen to present. Placing the presentation last happens for good reason. Prospects, buyers, and decision makers all consider it necessary to meet and listen to the winning seller or sales team. Even in an age where we communicate increasingly online rather than in person, people still want to meet and view sellers in person and base their buying decisions on first-hand observations.

As sellers present their ideas, decision makers seek to answer four key questions:

1. Does the seller's logic seem well thought out? People make this judgment based on how the content flows.
2. Does the seller appear assertive, bold, or confident? In other words, does he or she display a desire to "make it happen"? Viewers answer this question by observing the presenter's facial expressions, enthusiasm, and gestures.
3. Does the seller come across as sincere and trustworthy? The person's bearing, delivery, eye contact, or lack thereof reflects these character traits.
4. Does the individual reveal a creative side? That is, will the seller offer new insights to a problem or need? Screen visuals can be a key factor in evaluating the presenter's creativity.

Notice that viewers answer three of the questions by simply watching the seller. That's why presenters should be the most important part of the sale. In warfare if you command the high ground, you are in the superior position. If you're selling visually, you also dominate the high ground. In the following pages, we provide specific suggestions that will help you sell from the one-up position and gain the competitive advantage.

An Opportunity to Gain an Edge

Many salespeople are so in love with PowerPoint that they don't realize how it's crippling their selling efforts. Because it is so easy to use and takes so much of the work out of a pitch, relying on Power-Point seems like a no-brainer. We're suggesting that this is the perfect time to sell with brains—and with vision. An opportunity exists for any salesperson who recognizes the real value of visual selling. By drawing attention to yourself (or the seller) and shaping images, room environments, and physical appearance and gestures for maximum impact, you can capitalize on this opportunity.

Though you may recognize this opportunity or you would not have bought this book, many salespeople don't see it for two reasons:

1. Using PowerPoint text is like being offered a sample from a box of chocolate—it's very satisfying and you want more. By projecting the message on the screen, you don't even have to rehearse or worry about delivery skills. Just read away.

2. Some people are lazy. If you rely on PowerPoint exclusively, you probably don't want to make the effort that visual selling requires. It's not a huge effort, but it demands that you think about and plan all the visual aspects of your presentation.

A New Direction

To reap the rewards of visual selling, you must consider changes in your approach to persuading others. Some of you may already be good visual sellers and simply need to make incremental changes in your approach. Some of you may have to make more significant changes in order to benefit. Whatever your situation, this book provides you with ideas and tools to increase the effectiveness of your approach. It does not matter if you sell high-tech products one on one, low-tech supplies to groups of buyers, or professional services to corporate clients. Visual selling works for everyone.

To understand how it will work for you, let's preview the areas this book covers:

- *Recapturing center stage.* As we have emphasized, you cannot allow yourself to play second fiddle to PowerPoint text. For this reason, you must learn how to take center stage when you sell and turn the screen into a support medium. We discuss how you can co-exist with visuals and retain the prospect's focus.

- *Don't say what they see.* Even if you use PowerPoint less, you can still commit the sin of repeating whatever text appears on the screen. "Verbal mirroring" works directly against persuading prospects. Adults are insulted when sellers read aloud to them. They expect a more sophisticated presentation, and we talk about how to compliment what is seen with what is said.

- *The handout.* Besides ceding the focal point to PowerPoint and reading screen text, the third common visual mistake sellers make is improperly using handouts. With a handout, viewers don't even need to look up or listen to the seller. If you wish to sell successfully, you'll need to radically change your thinking on handouts and make them work for you instead of allowing them to upstage you.

- *The "right" visuals.* If you reject PowerPoint text, what could possibly take its place? The answer is images. A picture is worth a thousand words, and we explain how a well-chosen picture can be worth thousands of dollars in sales. We think, dream, and retain information in images, and we provide an explanation of why this is so and how you can capitalize on it when making a sale.

- *Choosing and using images.* How do you choose and use an image for maximum impact in a given selling situation? How do you find the visual that reinforces the messages you're delivering verbally? How often do you use an image, and when? We answer these and related questions, helping you sell with the right image in mind.

- *Supporting players.* In a game of chess, the pieces are always positioned to protect the king and queen. A parallel strategy applies to selling. Everything from the seller's clothes to the room set-up has a visual impact and must be controlled to support the seller. Rather than view these visual factors as inconsequential, sellers must understand their impact and control everything from where the presenter stands to how the screen is positioned and angled. We'll look at these and other ways you can exert visual influence on a sale.

- *The critical visual.* Finally, you'll have to master the most important visual of all—yourself. Few sellers realize the huge positive or negative influence that their body language broadcasts to viewers. Delivering a persuasive visual pitch requires as much physical finesse as playing a well-executed game of tennis or golf. Pros continuously work on their swing or follow-through to play a sport better. We examine how you can become more conscious of and control gestures and other aspects of body language to persuade others more effectively.

Visual Selling is divided into three parts: Part I explains the vital importance of positioning the seller as the focal point. If sellers don't hold complete viewer attention, they're seriously crippling their efforts.

Part II discusses how you prepare for a visual presentation and, in particular, how you incorporate images into your pitch.

We describe how to create a visual sequence for your pitch that takes full advantage of your new mastery of images.

In Part III, we look at a variety of selling situations involving groups of different sizes and interests. You'll understand what's visually important in a competitive presentation. You'll also learn how visual selling can dramatically enhance your booth at a convention and how it can reduce the electronic headaches that often plague road shows or heavy travel schedules. You'll read about a high-tech company that conveys its message to research scientists and consumers using image visuals and why the company founders credit a great deal of their success to visual selling.

As you'll discover, becoming well versed in the art of visual selling will benefit you in many ways. This book gives you the details on how to do everything from creating an original visual image to creating an effective selling environment whether you're at "home" or on the road.

We convey all this information using both words and images. Though books are a text medium, they can also take advantage of images as teaching tools, and you'll find more images in these pages than you would in other books on selling. These images reinforce the stories and specific techniques detailed in the text. You will see many examples of text slides converted to image visuals. At the end of this book, we hope you'll have a good understanding of the theory of visual selling and an even better grasp of how to put this theory into practice when you're trying to convince potential buyers.

The authors have been selling and advising others about how to sell for over 25 years. One author, Peg, has a great deal of sales and marketing experience in the investment field. The other, Paul, has specialized in competitive presentations since 1980.

We've watched the appalling growth and popularity of PowerPoint—the shift away from the presenter to prospects reading screen text and handouts. We've also witnessed how those who are overly reliant on PowerPoint text pitches often alienate customers and fail to make the sale. And we've seen that those who sell visually and keep the focus on themselves rather than screen are usually the ones who win in high-stakes, competitive presentations.

Finally, we'd like you to do a quick assessment of your current visual selling ability. Look at the following statements and note whether you agree or disagree with them:

- Use PowerPoint slides that bullet point your thoughts to keep you and your prospects or customers on track.
- Prepare a handout/deck so your listeners can follow along.
- For an important pitch, place the screen or your visuals in the middle of the room to highlight your information.
- Stand with your visual to your right.
- "Dress down" for a presentation because you don't want people to think you're too formal or what you're selling is too expensive.
- Turn off the room lights to ensure your screen information pops.
- Stand well to the side or sit at the table with your laptop so your slides receive maximum attention.
- If you stand, use few gestures because they are distracting and shift the focus away from your visuals.
- Use an electronic pointer because it helps direct the viewers.
- On a raised platform in a large meeting room, place your lectern to the side, well away from the screen.

The more of these statements you agree with, the less effective you will be as a visual seller. Don't be alarmed if you found yourself in agreement with some or all of the statements. Most salespeople and presenters operate under numerous misconceptions about what does and does not work from a visual standpoint. Correcting these visual errors requires acquiring a bit of information and applying it to a variety of presentation and selling situations. The following pages will communicate that visual knowledge and help you apply it so that you can persuade with greater effectiveness.

Acknowledgments

We want to thank our agent, Bruce Wexler, for his help in shaping this book and for his extraordinary editing. We are also grateful to Constance Lee Trojnar-Gauba for her ingenious and creative images that aptly illustrate the visual sell approach. Both individuals have been critical in bringing this book into being.

The Seller as Focal Point

CHAPTER

1

What Is Your Buyer Looking At?

"The soul never thinks without a picture."

—Aristotle, from his *De Anima*

You would think that any seller with a healthy ego would want to be the focus of a buyer's attention. You would assume that no seller wants to play second fiddle to a screen. Unfortunately, many sellers are perfectly willing to serve as a visual afterthought. They rationalize this secondary role 100 different ways, but it all boils down to the ease of using text on the screen.

If this describes your approach, you may have done so believing that "good" or "the right" information sells itself. If you are convinced that information sells, why bother verbalizing your ideas? Just put what you want to say in writing. It would save everybody an enormous amount of time.

We're assuming that no matter what your selling approach was in the past, you've recognized that words alone are not enough. When you've reflected on your selling experiences, you know that no idea sells itself. If words alone did the trick, religious groups wouldn't bother sending a multitude of missionaries to convert prospects. They would simply hand out bibles and let the "good book" do the selling.

Before we explain how to take advantage of visual selling, we need to convince you that you should be the main visual. Let's look at some powerful arguments that help make this point, starting with how your visuals should support you rather than vice versa.

The Most Important Visual

The seller must do the selling. This is not a task to delegate to a screen or hand out. You possess the experience and the expertise, the style and the savvy that will appeal to a prospect. You are much more likely to close the sale than an inanimate object. To sell your idea, all eyes must be focused on you. This means you must give prospects a compelling reason to look at you and make sure your visual support intensifies rather than diminishes this focus. In terms of this latter point, your visual support must fulfill the following criteria:

- *Hold viewer attention only briefly.* If prospects concentrate primarily on a screen, flip chart, poster board, or prop, the seller becomes secondary.
- *Allow sellers to deliver the message.* When text slides communicate the main selling points, they make presenters almost unnecessary. The ideal visual permits the seller to unfold the news and control the flow of information.
- *Reinforce the sale.* Slide-reading and paraphrasing hinders viewer retention. The visual must reinforce, not compete with, the seller's words.

Images, not text, place the seller back in visual control. Let's look at some examples that illustrate this truism.

Smoking Slide Example

Assume you're a Canadian MD, PhD, and research director, delivering a keynote presentation on the hazards of smoking to American insurance executives. Your laboratory has gathered over-whelming evidence that cigarettes make smokers impotent.

This presentation is excellent PR for your laboratory and could bring your firm more research work. Therefore, you want to make a powerful presentation that sells your audience. Naturally, you consider a presentation that uses standard text slides (Figure 1.1).

It dawns on you, however, how powerful images are. Also, you decide to unveil the findings yourself and not have the slide preempt your flow. For your first image, you choose a visual from the Canadian government's anti-smoking campaign that looks like Figure 1.2.

After you project the above slide and pause, you say: "Cigarettes can cause sexual impotence due to a decreased blood flow. Our three-year study reveals that . . ."

Let's look again at the three criteria. First, does the image hold viewers' attention only briefly? Will people be reading text or looking at and listening to the presenter? Second, who delivers the news, the slide or the speaker? Third, which slide reinforces

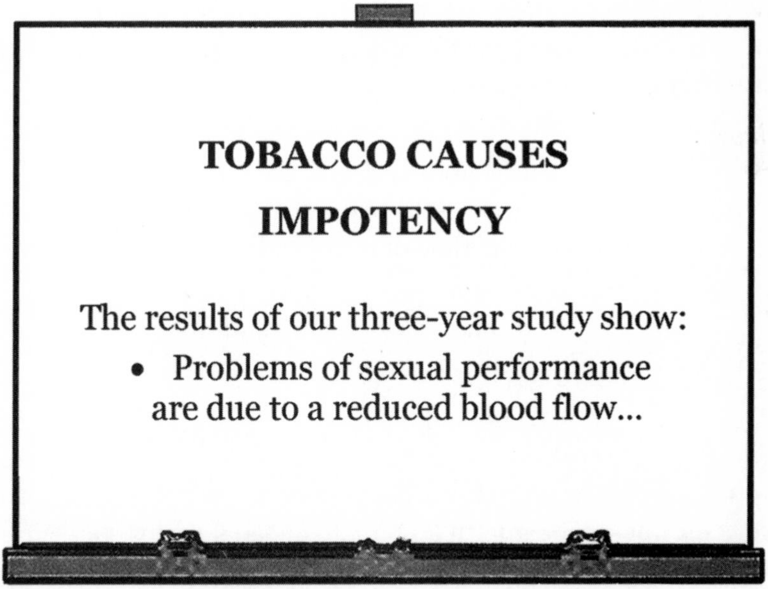

Figure 1.1 Impotency Text Slide

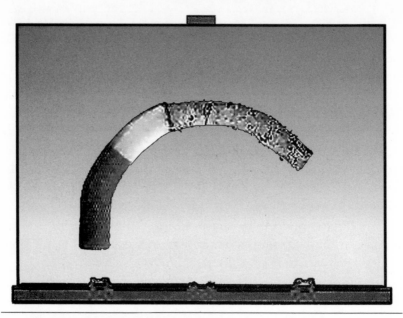

Figure 1.2 Impotency Image Slide (*Source:* http://www.hc-sc.gc.ca/ahc-asc/media/photogal/label-etiquette/index_e.html)

the message? Are these insurance executives likely to remember the text or the cigarette image a month later when they're discussing who to hire to conduct a new research project?

Canada requires cigarette packages to contain anti-smoking health warnings with images as well as text. Figure 1.3 is one of the graphics from their website.

The Canadian government mandates images to support cigarette labeling because extensive research studies show they increase the effectiveness of the message. For example, when subjects viewed a warning text alongside a photo of an emphysema lung, 72 percent chose the photo-based warning as more discouraging of smoking, 11 percent said text, and 12 percent said neither. The larger photo-based warnings were found to be even more effective among youths than adults. A full 88 percent of young people chose the warning with a photo, compared with 7 percent for text, and 4 percent for neither (Canadian Cancer Society media release, 2000).

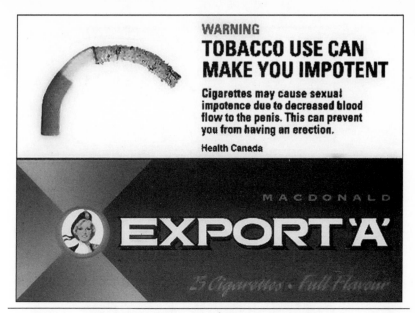

Figure 1.3 Canadian Cigarette Package

Images and photos can support your selling just as effectively. When the impotency concept floods the screen as a text slide, the presenter is merely a bystander. With the image slide, the speaker stands tall as a doctor, scientist, and persuader, but most of all, as the focal point. The presenter returns to the role of leading, explaining, and convincing.

Text Versus Images: Can You Identify the Salespeople Who Remain in the Spotlight?

Consider the following four slides, as shown and discussed by four presenters. Which visuals hold viewers' attention only briefly and allow the seller to deliver the news?

Figure 1.4 Retirement Reality

Presenter One

The first seller, a financial planner, displays the above slide (Figure 1.4) to a group in their mid-forties, pauses, and then says, "When you retire, you may be in for a rude shock. Statistics reveal that over half (the presenter points to the 57 percent) of retirees found they must continue working to maintain their previous lifestyles. Not only does their retirement income fall short, but also their new jobs rarely match previous responsibilities. They now find themselves selling fries or stocking shelves."

Presenter Two

The second seller, also a financial planner, addresses a group of mid-thirty year olds. He reads word for word from the screen (Figure 1.5), saying, "Unfortunately, most workers have no safety net. Seventy-one percent of white collar workers over 45

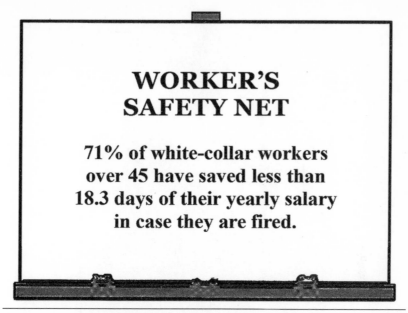

Figure 1.5 Worker's Safety Net

have saved less than 18.3 days of their yearly salary in case they are fired."

Presenter Three

While the screen is blank, a third presenter states, "As you know, being the head of human resources, I was asked to evaluate how we could recapture our position on the 100 Best Companies list."

On the screen pops an image with the words "100 Best" (Figure 1.6). The presenter continues, "It was unfortunate last year that we lost our footing on this prestigious list. We recommend improvements in three areas."

On the screen, three more images appear. Pointing to each in turn, the presenter says, "The three I'll be discussing are enhancing our childcare facility, providing more job rotation, and increasing work-hour choices. Now let me get into the details. First, our childcare . . ." This presenter never reads from the screen.

Figure 1.6 100 Best Image Slide

Presenter Four

A fourth presenter, also a human resources executive, hits the clicker and the title, "How to attract . . . ," and the first bullet point, "Provide a fuller . . ." becomes visible (Figure 1.7).

The presenter then says, "As you know, being the head of HR, I was assigned to try and figure out (He turns his back to listeners and reads from the screen.) how to attract better employees and get back on the 100 Best Companies list. It was unfortunate last year we lost our footing on this prestigious list. First, we'd recommend (Again he turns away from the listeners and reads from the screen.) providing a fuller range of daycare programs . . ."

As you can see, image slides do a better job of managing an audience's attention. With image slides, people look at the screen momentarily then quickly shift their focus to the presenter. Just as you read the two text slides, so will the audience at a presentation.

> ## HOW TO ATTRACT BETTER EMPLOYEES AND GET BACK ON THE 100 BEST COMPANIES LIST
>
> - **Provide a fuller range of daycare programs**
> - **Offer better flex hours to a wider range of employees**
> - **Rotate job responsibilities to keep key employees challenged**

Figure 1.7 100 Best Text Slide

Clearly, images satisfy the first two criteria for an ideal visual—holding listener attention briefly and allowing seller to control the flow of information.

Remembering the Message

Let's now examine the third criteria for an ideal visual—retention. Keeping your message alive in the prospect's mind is critical in promoting a positive buying memory. Do text or image slides do a better job of driving retention? Or look at this question another way: Are you more likely to remember the screen-projected words of a presenter or an image slide with the seller delivering the meaning that fills in the visual?

To help yourself answer this question, try and recall the details of the first two slides in this series of four. Even if you cruised through the last four slides quickly, you had no distractions. A speaker wasn't reading or paraphrasing the information while you were absorbing the slides or reading the text. The first slide dealt with working after retirement, and the second was about workers saving money. Take a moment and reproduce both slides on paper.

Our experience and a wealth of research say you'll remember much of the image slide—the older worker serving fast food and even the number 57. But chances are you can reconstruct little or none of the text slide—"71 percent of white-collar workers over 45 have saved less than 18.3 days of their yearly salary in case they are fired."

Given this retention exercise outcome, consider these points:

- You're an ideal viewer. You are awake and attentive.
- You just viewed the material, so retention is the highest it's ever going to be.
- You were asked to recall only two slides.

Under these ideal conditions, the retention of only one text slide is minimal. Did you even remember its title?

In real-life situations, a seller operates in far from ideal conditions. People aren't always attentive. They are often thinking about their workload, their personal lives or phone calls to make after they're done meeting with you.

Given these realities, why would a presenter show 20, 30, or even 50 text slides? If the message of one text slide can't be retained, then 20 to 50 such slides will merge into a truly unmemorable mass.

Researchers tell us the mind stores and retrieves pictures more efficiently than words. A face is easier to remember and recall than a name. Cognitive psychologists call this phenomenon the "picture superiority effect." Though researchers have not determined exactly why this phenomenon exists, some psychologists attribute it to the theory that images are remembered both as words and shapes. Others speculate that the unique shapes of graphics might be a superior memory hook.

Whatever the cause, research demonstrates that pictures are easier to recall than words, in both the short term and the long term. In one study, subjects recognized 612 pictures with 98 percent accuracy in the short term and even recognized 58 percent of them after 120 days (Shepard, 1967). In another by the same researcher, participants shown 2,560 images over several days recognized 90 percent of them. In a third concerning 10,000 pictures, subjects could both remember and recognize pictures more easily than words. After seeing them just once, they remembered pictures with surprising accuracy for as long as three months (Higbee, 2001, pp. 64–78). Some researchers speculate that human beings may have an almost unlimited capacity to remember pictures.

Images, therefore offer a *huge* retention advantage to those competing against sellers using text visuals.

When the Visual and Auditory Messages Are Out of Synch

To help a prospective buyer retain your sales message, you may read the words that appear on a screen. Your assumption is that reading what a prospect is seeing reinforces the message. In fact, it distorts the message, garbling the transmission.

Average readers zip along at 250 to 300 words per minute (wpm). Fast readers easily hit 600 to 800 wpm. But a presenter can speak no faster than 160 words per minute. Therefore, people can and will mentally read much faster than a presenter can speak.

When sellers read aloud, prospects are forced to struggle with a very disjointed message. Their ears hear the speaker while their eyes are scanning way ahead. It's hard to think of a worst way to process information than reading and hearing an out-of-synch voice. Try it with someone. It's extremely difficult to concentrate. Besides, why read or paraphrase visuals unless viewers are illiterate? Why risk sending the message to prospects that you think they're not bright enough to "get it" unless you read what they can't? Again, this approach moves the focus to the words on the screen, encouraging people to read rather than pay attention to you.

Repositioning Handouts

Handouts also drag people's eyes away from you. Imagine sitting in front of your boss's desk, asking for a much-deserved raise. Your sales volume tops the list, so you richly deserve a substantial increase. For a few minutes, your boss looks right at you, paying complete attention. Then he or she opens a report and starts turning the pages, glancing at you only occasionally. You would be furious. Not only is this rude behavior, but the boss is also missing large parts of what you're saying.

Now translate this scenario to a sales pitch. Consider what happens when you hand prospective buyers a brochure or other type of reading material. Naturally, their focus will drift to what you handed them. If you create a document—especially one that is colorful and eye-catching—they will invariably look at it. By avoiding handing out any material when you're speaking, you retain your prospects' attention except for those moments when you direct them to an image on a screen.

Companies often use the term "deck" to mean a document containing a printout of all the slides used during the presentation. It is distributed beforehand so listeners can follow along. If the deck is passed out after the presentation, it is usually referred to as a "handout." While it's fine to use the deck as a handout after the presentation is over, using it simultaneously is even worse than a simple handout because there is much more material to distract your prospective buyers' attention. Nothing you do will mutilate your message more than having prospects leaf through a deck while you sell. The moment you pass out a deck, you lose control. Prospects are torn three ways: they can flip through the deck, read what's on the screen, or listen to you. The deck is a sure winner; the seller is a sure loser.

Don't compete with simple handouts or more complex decks. You'll bet against yourself and lose.

Don't Fall for PowerPoint's Allure

Finally, we want to issue another PowerPoint warning. As many times as we advise our clients against relying on PowerPoint, we find that they are sometimes drawn to its use against their better judgment. PowerPoint text is like an outdoor light that attracts moths, and then destroys them. Like moths, sellers are drawn to PowerPoint's brilliance. Creating text with PowerPoint is easy and the finished product looks professional. There are colored backgrounds, fancy type styles, words that enter the screen turning and spinning. Background noise adds to the sensory appeal of the type and a sprinkling of clip art fosters the illusion that you're using images effectively.

Unfortunately, PowerPoint, like decks, handouts, and reading to your prospects, is a trap that's easy to fall into. The software lures people with the promise that a pitch will be easier to deliver and more effective. Moths feel equally drawn to the light until they slam into the bulb. It's too bad sellers don't find themselves stunned and flopping around on the floor. Fortunately, however, unlike moths, most sellers are capable of learning from their mistakes.

The first lesson we hope you've learned is to grab the prospect's visual attention and keep it. Once you've done that, the next step is polishing your visual self so that prospects like what they see.

CHAPTER

2

Now That You Have Their Attention, What Should You Do?

"There's a geometric progression in ability: you need to be only 10 percent better at what you do than most people in order to go 100 percent further."

—Sydney J. Harris, syndicated columnist

Since we've shifted the focus back to you and away from the screen, you don't want to present a boring or off-putting image. When you're in the spotlight, you want to make the most of it. You want to hold people's attention so their minds don't wander. To sustain attention and positive involvement, you have a number of techniques available to you. We'll examine these techniques, but first we'd like to share some examples of how sellers inadvertently make their viewers as nervous as they are.

What's Wrong with This Seller?

The toughest deal usually involves selling to a group. For example, you're in a final presentation run-off. You'll face only five decision makers, but they will determine your success or failure. As your stress level jumps, you rise and start your pitch. The pressure to "sell this big one" usually creates an adrenaline surge. The body says, "Go for it! Here's an energy shot." Unfortunately, this boost leads to visual hyperactivity that hurts rather than helps the sale. You step backward and forward or shift from one foot to the other. Your hands also want something to do—turn the wedding ring, wring the hands, or play "pocket pool." All these movements send the wrong visual message, suggesting you're anxious or uncertain about the ideas you're pitching (Figure 2.1).

If the stakes are high enough, your body probably feels like a shaken soda can. You're ready to explode. Unfortunately, the

Figure 2.1 Negative Gestures—Hiding Hands

adrenaline often pops the lid, resulting in negative gestures such as clasping or hiding your hands (Figure 2.2).

Sometimes it goes terribly wrong. A senior vice president for marketing of a major public company stood before some 700 stockholders to explain why last year's sales tanked. Naturally, he was nervous. His reputation was riding on his ability to offer a credible explanation for the bad year. He stood rigidly with his palm covering his groin. One hand tightly gripped his other wrist. This fig-leaf-like, protective gesture would have been bad all by itself. However, his anxiety made it worse. As the senior vice president spoke, one hand kept waving up and down (Figure 2.3). Obviously, he didn't realize what he was doing or what message this gesture was sending to the audience.

Everyone experiences some degree of anxiety when they're selling, especially when it's a potentially big sale with significant

Figure 2.2 Negative Gestures—Hands in Pockets

Figure 2.3 Groin Waving

consequences to your income and career. You can't stop your adrenaline from pumping but you can stop it from detracting from the image you're presenting. If you're conscious of it and know what to do about it, you can channel it in a positive direction. Here's how.

Step 1: Stand Your Ground

Plant yourself with your weight equally distributed and your feet apart, the same width as your shoulders. Slightly bend you knees. A basketball or football player on defense uses the same stance. This position applies to both man and women. You're ready to react in any direction, except you won't react with your feet (Figure 2.4).

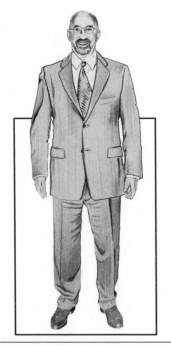

Figure 2.4 Seller in Correct Neutral Position

Figure 2.5 Incorrect—The Leaner or Pacer

Some argue that taking a few steps while talking helps burn off nervousness. You could justify the same for wringing the hands or playing with a wedding ring. All these movements represent anxiety driving the presenter rather than the seller using anxiety in a positive way.

You must stay planted while channeling all your nervous energy to your arms and face. That's where you want the visual attention—not below the belt in leg movements such as shifting or pacing (Figure 2.5).

After you ground yourself, place your arms straight down at your sides. Don't put your hands in your pockets. There are too many stories of presenters playing with pocket change while audiences hide their smirks (Figure 2.6).

Figure 2.6 Incorrect—Pocket Jammer

Step 2: Gesture Correctly

Few keep their hands in their pockets when giving directions.

—Anonymous

The objective is to channel the energy, not hold it back. Gestures are an excellent way to burn adrenaline. First let's consider how gestures enhance your visual appearance; then we'll discuss how to gesture. The specific benefits of gesturing are:

- *Burning off energy:* Instead of fidgeting or making inappropriate movements, gestures provide a positive outlet for your increased energy.
- *Looking professional:* Gestures, executed correctly, become positive movements instead of negative, embarrassing ones. The right gestures can convey confidence and commitment to your prospects and customers.
- *Supporting the message:* It's not uncommon for gestures, even more than words, to carry the message. Think of an obscene gesture. It can enrage the viewer. More subtly, a supportive gesture emphasizes the importance of a point.
- *Involving listeners:* When sellers gesture, people pay attention. Instead of staring at a photograph, they're watching a movie. Viewers find it mentally hard to turn away from the "action."
- *Slowing down:* Gestures help you slow down. It takes a half-second to match the words to the gesture. Without gestures, your verbal pace often accelerates. You won't even notice that you're talking too fast. Words backed with deliberate gestures force you into a slower, conversational pace.

With these benefits in mind, be conscious of your use of "size and action" words, and the opportunity to reinforce these words with gestures:

- *Size:* You simply talk and gesture to descriptive words (Figures 2.7 through 2.9). It's a big, small, wide, thick, tall, short . . .

Figure 2.7 We Estimate
a *Small* Cost for the
Initial Project

Figure 2.8 Profits Are
Sinking to a New
Low Point

Figure 2.9 The Margins Are *Huge*

- *Action:* When you talk, you can't help but use action verbs. For instance: "About one in every eight words we *say*, *reflects* action. You can *bet* on that. *Try* it yourself. You'll easily *hit* one in eight." (Action verbs italic.) (See Figures 2.10 through 2.13.)

Exercises to Put Your Gestures into Practice

Will gestures come naturally? No, especially if you've spent years resisting these movements. For most people, gesturing is a learned skill. You must practice speaking and physically expressing the words at the same time. Here are some guidelines to help:

- *Be specific.* Avoid vague gestures. Instead, create gestures to match a specific word or phrase. Consider correct and incorrect gestures to accompany "We are *heading* for a successful completion" in Figures 2.14 and 2.15.

Figure 2.10 Your Sales
Will *Skyrocket*

Figure 2.11 Allan Will *Analyze*
the Data

Figure 2.12 We Need to
Check off Results

Figure 2.13 I'll *Focus* on
Improvements

Figure 2.14 Heading
for—Correct

Figure 2.15 Heading
for—Incorrect

- *Oversize your gestures.* Gestures used in front of the group must be larger than those used in one-to-one situations. When selling your ideas to a group, keep your gestures chest level, a good foot away from your body and oversized. The greater the distance you are from your group or the larger the group, the more exaggerated the gestures.

- *Get your timing right.* Don't rush your gesture. Don't just throw it out there. Milk its value. You've created a compelling visual. Let it linger a second in the viewer's mind. If you're specific with gestures and give them the time they deserve, you'll slow yourself down, appear in control, come across as a polished presenter and reinforce your message.

- *Quantity counts, but so does quality.* You don't have to gesture like a symphony conductor to get your points across, but you do need to find a gesturing rhythm that suits you. As a general rule, shoot for a gesture with every third to fifth sentence. For example, a presenter says: "We need to *pull* the old price lists. *Throw* them out. *Rewrite* new ones. And then *send* them out to the field offices." Four gestures are possible. Find your comfort level and go with all four or only one. Don't go more than five sentences, however, without making a gesture.

- *Use more visual verbs.* Once you become aware of your verbs and react with gestures, you can increase the effectiveness of those gestures by using verbs with a stronger visual element. For example, let's look at two of the above seller's verbs:

  "*Pull* the old price list."

  "*Throw* them out."

  You'll intensify the imagery of both verbs by substituting the following:

  "*Yank* the old price list."

  "*Trash* them."

  Yank and trash sound more dramatic; consequently, your viewers will find it easier to envision what you're saying.

Think of the difference between "he went" versus "he strutted, slunk, or shuffled" across the room. Each conjures an image that is more powerful than "he went across the room."

- *Avoid only one-armed gestures:* Using only one-handed gestures looks halfhearted, weak, or limp. Watch folks during lunch or when they're standing and engaging in conversation. They gesture mostly with both hands—not one. "We need both a floor and a ceiling on this deal." Woman's hands positions north and south (Figure 2.16). "It's a huge mess." Woman's hands extending east and west. Or "Time is running out." Woman's one hand pointing to a wristwatch on her other hand (Figure 2.17).

Figure 2.16 Correct Two-Arm Gesture—Ceiling and Floor

Figure 2.17 Correct Two-Arm Gesture—Time Running Out

From Awkward to Natural

At first, incorporating these gestures into your sales pitches may seem phony. Part of the problem is that until you become comfortable with gesturing effectively, you'll experience a delay between the thought and the action. You'll tell yourself to make the gesture, and it emerges a bit behind the spoken words. You say, "There are two factors . . ." Then one second too late, you raise your hand and extend two fingers. The gesture feels awkward.

Expect your gestures to feel abrupt or time-delayed initially. Do not let this discourage you. For a beginner, it is difficult to step correctly into a tennis shot aimed at your face. Once mastered, though, you can return the shot in a fluid and easy motion. The same process takes place with gestures. With a little practice, gesturing will flow spontaneously.

Step 3: Display Enthusiasm Visually as Well as Verbally

People don't care how much you know unless they know how much you care.

—Jamie Humes, Presidential speechwriter

Enthusiasm is based on a Greek word that translates roughly as the god, the spirit, and the energy within you. We admire people who have high spirit and energy. Outstanding leaders motivate those around them with enthusiastic attitudes and actions. In convincing others, no visual element is more important than enthusiasm. Yet, it is the hardest of all delivery skills to learn or to teach.

Years ago when we coached executives for presentations, we often encouraged them to boost their enthusiasm. Typically, we would say, "Give it more heart, more feeling, more drama, or more passion." Nothing worked. Frustrated by their inability to do what we requested, we said, "Forget enthusiasm. Just speak louder."

Amazingly, it worked. Increase your volume and, like magic, enthusiasm usually appears. It is a direct one-to-one relationship. When you speak louder, you are also more likely to display body language that communicates your enthusiasm. At the same time, recognize that you are going to resist the increased volume and the enthusiastic body language that accompanies it.

Six factors work against anyone trying to produce enthusiasm: First, we are accustomed to the volume needed for one-to-one conversations. Therefore, our voice level is a deeply rooted habit. Second, when we are nervous, throat muscles tighten. To increase the volume we have to work against our body. That is not comfortable. Third, most people feel that the increase from "normal" to "loud" results in yelling. Of course, it does not, but that is the perception. Fourth, people who are nervous have a subconscious resistance to speaking louder, since it draws more attention to them. Fifth, most people believe a loud voice suggests that they are aggressive, obnoxious, or pushy. Sixth, your voice sounds louder than it actually is; people making presentations hear their own voices amplified not only through their ears, but also through the roof of their mouth and their facial bone structure. People who are listening to them, however, are much farther away and do not hear this amplification.

To get past these obstacles, try the following experiment to convince yourself how increased volume produces increased enthusiasm. Place a secretary, direct reports, or other associates in a rehearsal room, similar in size to the one in which you are going to deliver your pitch. After a few minutes, have someone else standing nearby whisper or signal to you to raise your volume. Have them repeat the signal several times. Raise your volume with each signal. Yes, louder than the last time. Then ask your observers what they thought of your normal speaking voice versus the louder versions. Invariably, they will tell you how much more enthusiastic you seemed "once you got going."

Be aware that enthusiasm conveys that you firmly believe in your idea. Enthusiasm only succeeds when *others* feel it, see it, and believe it. Dramatically stepping up your volume and keeping it there increases your chances for that to happen. Your audience or customers will see exciting facial expressions, more gestures, and hear the commitment in your voice.

Use a mirror or digital video recorder to check your stance or practice gestures. However, be especially vigilant about your tendency to speak softly. Show the video to or rehearse in front of people who will be honest about how you come across. Ask them if you seemed committed, energetic, and excited. Second, test three voice levels during these rehearsals—a conversational level, a persuasive level, and an overly loud level. This last level is not yelling, but it does require you to raise the volume to just below how your voice might sound when you are cheering for your favorite sports team.

Most people seriously underestimate how loud they need to speak to communicate enthusiasm. Understand that a normal speaking voice for one-to-one conversations carries less than 3 feet. The distance from you, to even a small group, can easily range from 10 to 15 feet or more. So just to be heard and register your energy and commitment, you must project your voice to a group at double or triple your normal speaking level.

If you're selling one on one, you don't want to shout out your pitch. Still, even one on one, you can increase your volume "subtly" to demonstrate that you believe in what you're selling. By speaking more distinctly and intensely, you increase your amplitude. Combined with small but well-timed gestures, this increased volume makes you a more effective one-on-one salesperson.

Microphones and Enthusiasm

We hope you are not thinking, "I don't need to worry about increasing the volume, because I use a microphone!" A microphone is a crutch that does absolutely nothing to produce enthusiasm. In fact, a microphone only magnifies a shaky or breaking voice. An unsteady voice is a dead giveaway that the presenter is nervous. Squeaky or fluttering voices are like negative gestures. Just as you gesture to burn adrenaline, you should also project a higher volume to burn nervousness. In fact, without sufficient volume, your voice is much more likely to crack and break.

Save the microphone for a large room with over 40 or even 50 people. With lesser numbers, stand tall, look at the person sitting farthest away, inhale deeply and project your most enthusiastic level. Then you will look and sound like you really care about the idea, service, or product you're pitching.

Impact Statements Guarantee Enthusiasm

Starting a pitch is tough. Tension has built up. You are unsure of yourself. A runner's leg may quiver as he or she crouches in the sprinter's block, but in a flash, as the starter's gun fires, all the nervousness burst into positive energy. Here is the equivalent to help you instantly take command, burn nervousness, and project a positive image. We call the technique an impact statement.

These statements combine the verbal with the visual. They also combine a number of our previous recommendations to help you convey a committed, excited attitude. As their name implies, impact statements make immediate and effective impressions on prospects and customers. To use this technique, you simply need to follow these three rules:

1. Limit the statement to five words or less.

2. Use a specific, supporting gesture.

3. Triple your normal speaking volume. (If you're selling one on one, vary your intonation to emphasize key points rather than raise the volume to the point you scare away the prospect on the other side of the desk.)

Let's say you are a HR consultant selling a service to help turn around employee morale. The first words out of your mouth, after you get the preliminary greetings and introductions out of the way, should be the impact statement. It officially starts your presentation. Here are three versions:

1. *Words:* "High turnover!" *Gesture:* Arm rising skyward.

2. *Words:* "Revolving door!" *Gesture:* Arm moving in circular motion.

3. *Words:* "You're pushing employees away!" *Gesture:* Palms up facing listeners, pushing toward them.

An impact statement immediately seizes listener attention and burns off your nervous energy. It grabs attention because you are upping the volume three levels. Both the intensified voice projection and your gestures allow you to burn adrenaline instantly.

Step 4: Pause Frequently

The notes I handle no better than many pianists. But the pauses between the notes—ah, that is where the art resides!

—Arthur Schnable, concert pianist

Pausing, along with eye contact (which we'll discuss next), are tougher to master than the previous three skills, since you will be going against the wishes of your own body, not merely redirecting energy. However, by exercising these two skills, you will put into play the strongest strength of all—self-control.

Of all the delivery skills, pausing will feel the strangest. Adrenaline throws you into overdrive. Why hold back when all systems race ahead? However, as the body speeds up, the chances for a crash dramatically increase. Pausing is not an option; it is a necessity.

Your body revs up for a good reason. For thousands of years, your ancestors fought saber tooth tigers and conquered neighboring tribes. They often walked around on high alert. Today, it still makes good sense for your unconscious to help you out—pump the adrenaline, rally the defenses. Self-preservation still rules. As you well know, some prospects and customers are biased or object irrationally. Your body normally does not differentiate between the lurking, potential street mugger and the individual asking tough or negative questions. For both, your unconscious releases the full shot of adrenaline. For most of us, when the body speeds up (faster voice, shifting feet, fidgeting hands, scanning eyes), stopping these accelerated actions with pauses seems unnatural.

The key, therefore, is to make a conscious effort to slow down through pauses. The first few minutes into your presentation, pause for two seconds after every sentence. For instance: "Hello." (one thousand one, one thousand two) "My name is Paul LeRoux." (one thousand one, one thousand two) "I'm here to convince you to pause." (one thousand one, one thousand two) "The good news is it isn't hard." (one thousand one, one thousand two) "Just follow one simple rule." (one thousand one, one thousand two) "After every sentence . . ."

Do this for five to eight sentences or more until you are very aware of your slow, deliberate pace. Wait until you feel you have a firm grip on yourself. Then ease up. Now proceed with a pause after every other sentence. (One thousand one, one thousand two) Continue until you are in control or your racing heart stops pounding.

If your speed increases, return to a pause every sentence or every other sentence. For example, let's say halfway through your presentation, the prospect's boss enters the room, scowls at you, looks at his or her watch, and then stares in your direction while leaning against the wall waiting for you to finish. Suddenly another bucket of adrenaline floods your system. Do not panic. Return to pausing after every sentence. You must control the adrenaline or you will react and be thrown.

Actually, you can slow yourself down two ways—pausing and eye contact—and they should be done in tandem.

Step 5: Make Eye Contact

To make oneself understood to people, one must first speak to their eyes.

—Napoleon Bonaparte

To look at everybody is to look at nobody. Scanning—taking in the entire group—is a deeply rooted, terrible habit. It probably started at an early age when we had to give our first stand up, grade school presentation. The teacher said, "Peg, when you face the class don't stare at your feet, glance at the ceiling or fiddle with your fingers. Instead involve the class by looking at them."

"Involve the class" rings true. "Looking at them" runs false. Before viewing your favorite TV program, position a lightweight chair three feet from the tube. Now try watching the TV and looking at the chair. Impossible, right? It's either the chair or the tube, not both. Pitching one on one or presenting to a group works the same way.

You can't see or connect with Jace if you are looking at Jennifer, Martha, and Mary. If you're scanning the group, you see nothing except a crowd. From Jace's viewpoint, you're certainly not connecting with him when your eyes scan the group.

When you scan a room, your brain is feverishly working three jobs: you're processing tons of visual information; you're struggling to choose the right words; and then you're worrying about the viewers' reactions. That's a heavy mental load. The faster and longer you scan, the greater the odds that the visual input will overwhelm your thought process and you'll blank out. As a listener, you've frequently seen a multitasking speaker hit the wall. A seller talks a mile a minute, wrings his hands, and rapidly eyes the room. Then the presenter suddenly stops and looks to the ceiling. You know what's happened. He has blanked out and forgotten what comes next. It often happens when the voice and the eyes speed up. The presenter's "slip" occurs because he or she has bombarded the brain with too many tasks—taking in images, threading the thoughts, and talking.

Scanning also breeds other negatives. Listeners feel neglected. Sellers who scan don't connect with their viewers. What would you think of a person who talks one to one but can't maintain eye contact for less than a second or two before glancing away? Insecure, impersonal, nervous, shifty, dishonest, or all of the above?

Correct Eye Contact

Good eye contact communicates a personal and sincere connection. To make good eye contact, though, you must deal with adrenaline that pushes the body to speed up. A speeding voice, fidgeting hands, shifting feet, and darting eyes are all part of your body's natural defense mechanism unless you make a hard choice to do something else.

Extended eye contact is a good antidote. Your eye movement regulates how quickly you speak and wring your hands. Scanning makes you talk and fidget faster. Therefore, slow your eye contact *waaay* down—an average of *three* seconds per face. Think average. You can look at John for only one second (one thousand one). However, to achieve your goal, you must look only at that next person's face for a full four seconds (one thousand one, one thousand two, etc.). In this way, you'll both engage each individual within the group and keep your voice and eyes under control.

Combining Eye Contact and Pausing

Now let's combine eye contact and pausing. After you deliver your impact statement, pause *two full seconds*, shift to a new face, and follow these rules:

1. Lock in with eye contact and *stay eyeball to eyeball* for three to five seconds. You may want to break away and glance at the ceiling or another person. Don't. With this first prospect or

customer, shoot for at least three to five seconds. This will force you to connect instead of prematurely jumping to the next person. In sum, lock eye contact for three to five full seconds as you talk to each person.

2. With the first and every person you're eyeing, force yourself to *finish your sentence* before you move to the next face. Be very hard-nosed with this rule and you'll achieve it 70 to 80 percent of the time. If you're not tough on yourself, you'll quickly slide to less than 20 or 30 percent, which is scanning. Finish your sentence before you move to the next face. Finish eye contact only at the end of each sentence.

3. *Pause* for one to two seconds as you shift to a new face. No talking. There is a powerful urge to keep jabbering as you move from face to face. That's the worst—blabbering combined with scanning. In short, go overboard with *pauses between faces.*

4. When you leave one face to go to the next, *aim for the person sitting farthest away* (assuming you're pitching to a group). The tendency is to shift quickly to the immediate left or right of the person you just looked at. If you do this, the pause will be only a split second. Instead, go slowly from one corner listener to the opposite corner listener. Now your pause hits a duration of one to two seconds. Always aiming for the greatest distance between faces also forces you to involve all areas of the group and not favor just people in the front or individuals you know.

Step 6: Be Clothes Conscious

> *Clothes make the man. Naked people have little or no influence.*
>
> —Mark Twain

Every pitch starts with your viewers forming a first impression. They see your face, body features, movements, and then your clothes. As you wade into your pitch, they continue their evaluation by judging your delivery skills, which we've just covered. Then they consider your clothes.

Clothes have always provided social clues to identity. For thousands of years, it was easy to distinguish the king or queen from the villagers because of the former wore crowns and colorful, highly designed outfits while the commoners wore dull, highly functional clothes. Little has changed. We immediately recognize the pimp in his orange suit and baggy pants; the factory worker in a darker shirt, jeans, and metal lunch box; the farmer in bib overalls; and the banker, lawyer, or accountant in a conservative pinstriped suit.

Your clothes can immediately "say" you are below average (denim), normal (cotton), or above average (linen, silk, or wool). Your clothes can make you appear slick or trying too hard or sloppy and not caring. Some people, of course, can get away with wearing what they want. Albert Einstein didn't comb his hair, let alone worry about his outfits. If you are the world's brightest, clothes don't matter. However, for the rest of us, what we wear reflects our educational, social, and economic level; it also suggests how dedicated we may be to serving a given customer, how we'll sweat the details and how we value quality.

Unfortunately, many sellers and presenters pay too little attention to their clothes. Here are three guidelines that will help you avoid this visual faux pas: It's better to be overdressed, it's wise to buy a few good pieces instead of many cheap ones and it's good to be cool.

Overdressed

Before the 1950s, you could divide the world into those who wore a tie and those who didn't—those who managed and those who worked the factory floor. The 1960s blurred that dividing line. Casual Fridays in the 1980s has become casual dress every day. Now more people wear denim and khaki than suits and ties, at least in most major cities. Even those in management often skip the jacket. Nonetheless, clothes still convey status.

Senior management usually suits up in designer clothes with extra touches like pocket scarves; rich, colorful ties; and expensive wristwatches. Those holding top positions and wielding power are men and women wearing woolen pinstripes, not jeans. There are exceptions (such as in dot-com companies), but in top management, designer suits far outnumber denim or cotton wearers.

Therefore, wear "power suits" and other outfits that are formal and stylish when you are making an important pitch. Even if you walk in and your prospect is sporting a polo shirt, you're better off in a jacket. You're saying, "This occasion deserves my best." It's always better to over dress than risk under dressing.

Quality Counts

Coco Channel, the famous French designer, advised women to start life buying books, art, and one good black dress. For both sexes, it's better to buy one good quality, conservative suit than two cheap things.

Yes, quality always costs more. You're paying for design creativity and workmanship. That's why these clothes fit better and feel better. Consequently, you'll feel better about yourself and reflect that to your listeners. Invest in yourself.

Don't devalue the quality image by wearing an old shirt or blouse. Nothing beats the crispness of a new one. The color, especially a white shirt, is the brightest, freshest it will ever be before the laundry knocks it down. Be elegant. Reflect class. Wear quality.

When you stand to convince, viewers may have no idea about your education or social standing. Nevertheless, in seconds, they will come to some opinion. People will more easily form a positive impression if you dress well.

Stay Cool

Pitching your ideas, products, or services and persuading individuals to buy them invariably raises stress levels. You'll feel warmer, your heart races and you may perspire. Your clothes can add to this problem. In the winter, for an important pitch, you may choose to wear a vested suit or that beautiful but heavy, tweed sports jacket. Don't. Your vest or tweedy jacket will only trap body heat and add to your perspiration problems.

Instead, even in the winter, wear lightweight, worsted wool whether it's a sport jacket, slacks or a suit. Lightweight wool breathes nicely. During January in Chicago, you'll need a heavy overcoat to stop the wind from knifing through your tropical wool attire. However, once you arrive to deliver your important pitch, your summer outfit will ventilate especially well and look great.

Be comfortable and familiar with your clothes. Don't wear an outfit for the first time when important prospects will be staring at you. First, test-drive the whole ensemble. Go out for a meal, a movie, or at least a cup of coffee. Careful about spills! Get used to the fit. How will it feel to raise your arms, gesture, or point to the screen? You don't want to feel like a small child crammed into a snowsuit where every movement feels constrained.

Delivery Is the Sum of Its Parts

Just wearing the right clothes isn't enough. Neither is exhibiting enthusiasm. Instead, people will judge you on how consistently and well you incorporate all six of the steps we've outlined. If you shift nervously back and forth while you're speaking, it's not going to matter that you speak in a loud, enthusiastic manner. You must execute all six elements well to achieve a total visual impact.

The good news is that none of these skills is particular tough to master. Some take practice. Some simply require you to spend a little money (clothes). When you stand to present in front of a group or sit down to sell one on one, you will look like you know what you're doing. You're going to convey the impression that you're sincere, confident, and committed. That impression will go a long way toward influencing the sale.

3

Q&A: Thinking Visually and Verbally in Post-Pitch Situations

"It's better to ask some of the questions than to know all the answers."

—James Thurber, U.S. humorist and cartoonist

As we've emphasized, you should be the focal point, whether you're selling one on one or making a pitch to a group. What happens, however, when you open things up for questions? How can you maintain the spotlight when your prospect starts talking?

Contrary to conventional wisdom, you're not giving up the floor just because you're accepting questions. If the group loses focus because you allow the person asking the question to take over, then you have no one to blame if you lose the sale. You can maintain visual control even during question and answer (Q&A) sessions. Let's look at the different ways you can do so.

Promoting Questions
with a Summary

Before asking for questions, make sure you summarize your pitch. Start your summary with the words, "In summary" or "In conclusion." This is a crucial step that many salespeople often skip and simply end their prepared presentation by abruptly asking, "Any questions?" Salespeople who fail to give their audience time to formulate questions often don't receive any. And that's a shame. Q&A offers a great selling opportunity, especially if you manage the visual aspects of this postpresentation session.

A summary accomplishes two things: First it neatly and quickly ties up your message, especially for those who may have mentally drifted during your pitch. Second, a summary provides time for your listeners to think of questions and gather their courage to ask. Also by offering a compelling summary, you'll promote more pertinent questions.

Getting Too Personal

A big mistake is to believe that those who ask questions warrant personalized attention. This is a bad visual strategy unless it's a one-on-one pitch. The salesperson must act like a pilot. The captain is responsible for all the passengers—certainly not a single individual or just the first-class passengers. If you concentrate only on the questioner, you risk losing the visual attention of everyone else. In addition, if you favor the questioner, you're saying to the group, "This person is more important than you." Usually several other people have the same thought in mind. The questioner simply acts as the spokesperson for the group.

During Q&A, you must involve the group. This assumes that most or all of the people you're addressing will have some input into the decision you want them to make. Be aware, however, that your instincts will lead you to focus on the individual rather than the group during Q&A. We're so used to talking one to one—directing our full attention to a single individual—that we naturally concentrate on the questioner.

Your visual efforts and words during Q&A must focus on the group. Therefore, the advice that follows promotes involving all the people in the room, not just the questioner.

The Transition

The transitional period between the end of your presentation and the beginning of questions is crucial. You want to give people as much time as possible to formulate their questions and you also want to maintain the visual connections you've worked hard to establish during this segue. Here are three transition techniques to achieve this goal:

1. *Most frequently asked:* Start with the words, "Before I answer your questions, let me tell you that the most frequently asked question I receive in presenting this idea/service/product is . . ." In a way, you're priming the pump with this technique; you essentially are asking the first question. More than that, though, by sharing with your audience the most popular question, you're keeping their gaze fixed on you. Clearly, you're conveying important information by telling them the most asked question and providing them with the answer.

2. *The survey:* "Before I answer your questions, let me take a quick survey. How many of you have . . . ?" Be sure to feed the results of the survey back to the group. Those sitting in front can't always see which hands behind them are raised. Again, this is a highly visual interaction. Briefly, people will stop looking at you to see who else is raising his or her hand. Then, when you tell them the results of your informal survey and its significance—you're in the best position to interpret the results—all eyes will snap back to you.

3. *Your concern:* "Before I answer your questions, let me say that if your concern is still . . ." Here you plug in the problem you

believe might be lingering—price, delivery, the downtime for the conversion, and so on. You quickly refer to the point you made when presenting about why the high cost is well worth it or how the conversion and short downtime will be pain-free, and so on. Again, this isn't tangential to your pitch; you're keeping everyone from lapsing into postpitch apathy or impatience. This is a key point, one they're concerned about, so as soon as you use the "concern" word, they'll be paying attention to you. Also you are channeling their thoughts toward the most pertinent question—their concern. It's your last chance to ensure your pitch answered a main objection.

Encouraging Questions

Certainly, an inviting, positive tone will encourage people to ask questions. Say just, "Questions!" It's easier to project a positive, strong voice with only one word. There are two problems with longer versions like, "Are there any questions?" First, this sounds as if you doubt there are any questions or don't want questions. Second, with multiple words, your voice can more easily slide into a nervous or demeaning tone. Beyond what you say and how you say it, don't forget to invite questions visually. Here are two techniques that will prompt questions:

1. *Your arm:* As you say, "Questions," fully raise one arm in a symbolic gesture, demonstrating what you hope they'll do. This gesture tells listeners three things: you are looking for their participation, you are suggesting they mirror your gesture to ask a question rather than blurt it out, and you are in control because you'll decide who talks. Keep your arm up.

2. *Your eyes:* Start by looking at the extreme right or left side of the group. Then slowly move your face and eyes across the viewers. This implies you are seeking questions from everyone. If you started on the left, continue to the extreme right. Move your eyes slowly, and then reverse direction, but slowly.

This gives people plenty of time to have the courage to raise their hands. Keep your hand up and remain silent. This places the burden on someone in the group to respond. The silence makes the group slightly uncomfortable. Therefore, someone will raise his or her hand simply to break the tension. Remember, we're only talking about three to five seconds of silence to encourage questions. Don't panic. Hold your ground. Smile and keep your hand up.

Bide Your Time

As the first hand rises, don't acknowledge that person immediately. Continue your full sweep—left to right, then right to left. This very short wait accomplishes two things: more hands may rise and you can decide which hand to pick. You are assessing whether the questioner is a friend or foe.

It's always risky to point to a hand that shoots up immediately just as Q&A starts. That individual is probably eager to nail you. Instead, after the full sweep, start with a friendly face, if one exists. Of course, you'll eventually have to acknowledge the potential hostile questioner. But it's better to start on firm ground with a friendly or more neutral question. Then go with the tougher one after you feel more confident.

Your Response

Once you have decided to acknowledge the first question, lower your arm, point to him or her, and say one of three things: "Yes," "Question," or the questioner's name. Only say the person's name if you know everybody in the group. Otherwise you'll say, "uhhh, yes," thereby acknowledging that you didn't bother to remember or learn that person's name.

Visually, it's important that you not step toward the questioner, even though you'll have a strong urge to do so. Stand your ground. If you move toward the questioner, you'll also look at and talk only to him or her. You *don't* want to go one to one. Your responsibility is to the group, not the questioner. If you are selling one on one, you may want to edge forward in your chair in response to the other individual's question. In group situations, though, don't lose the group for the sake of one person.

Doesn't this advice alienate the person with the question? Not if you use the following technique. When you decide whose question you want to answer, lower your arm with an open palm and gesture in that person's direction. (No finger pointing.) Then give 100 percent of your eye contact to the questioner. You're implying that you are hanging on every word that he or she is saying, which is exactly what you should be doing.

When the questioner stops talking, return your eye contact to the group. Your first and most important visual move here is to shift your eyes to the person farthest from the questioner. Second, repeat the question. Third, move your eyes among the group as you answer the question. Fourth, don't end with your eye contact back on the questioner.

Let's look at these four priorities in detail:

1. *Move your eyes away.* When the questioner finishes speaking, you must move your eyes away or you'll lock eyes with the questioner and slide into a one to one instead of talking to the group. No, the questioner won't feel slighted. He or she intuitively understands that you need to involve the group.

2. *Repeat the question.* While this is not technically a visual selling step, repeating a question is usually a guaranteed way to draw everyone's attention to you as the authority rather than toward the questioner. You reassert your focal prominence when you repeat a query and have a chance to take the following four positive actions:

   a. Makes sure everyone has heard the questions. Sellers often assume falsely that everybody heard the remark. The questioner faces the seller, so the voice sounds loud enough, but behind that person or to the side, the questioner's voice may not project well.

   b. Allows the seller to hear the question again and think about it. Repeating the question often causes the seller to respond with a more correct or appropriate answer rather than blurting out an emotional reply. Good politicians do this all the time. The questioner will ask, "What do you think of Richard Nixon?" The politician will respond, "Hum, Nixon (pause) . . . ?" Obviously, the politician is forming a "politically correct" response.

c. Offers the opportunity to shorten or rephrase the question in a more positive light. For example, the questioner says, "Well, you know, we are operating on a tight budget. Every dollar counts. Why do we have to waste money on this repair?" You could repeat the question with something as simple as, "Cost?" Or use a little looser version with, "Justifying a repair?" Keep your interpretive repeat short and neutral if possible. In some instances, though, you'll need to offer a slightly longer, positive interpretation, such as, "The question of repair cost raises the importance of preventive maintenance."

d. As much as possible, try and strip the negative out of the question in your repeated form. For example, the question is, "Why is your delivery time so long?" Your response, "The question is our delivery schedule?" Or the tighter version, "Delivery time?" Or a positive interpretation, "The question is, the time needed to tailor your system before we ship?"

3. *Answer the question with your eyes and a pause.* As you talk, what you do with your eyes is almost as important as what you say. Before you utter the first word of your response, you must turn your head and eyes away from the questioner. Your reflex will be to look at the questioner as you reply—not looking at the other person in one-to-one conversations is rude. In this context, however, it is not rude, since everyone recognizes your responsibility and communication is to the group.

When the questioner finishes, pause for two seconds. This allows questioners to add another thought if he or she wishes. The point is you want to know, if possible, the person's intent before you respond. That's good poker, especially if the person blurts out something negative.

If the questioner doesn't jump in during the pause, move your head and eyes to the person sitting on the opposite side and the farthest distance from the questioner. This prevents you from talking one to one. Now follow your normal eye contact pattern. Remember, good eye contact is both the three-second average per listener and moving your eyes throughout the group.

4. *Move your eyes away again.* As you finish answering the question, you must *not* end your words while looking at the questioner. This invites the questioner to jump in with a rebuttal or follow up to your answer. Instead, end your eye contact on the person farthest away from the questioner.

Not ending your eye contact on the questioner does not imply that you shouldn't give the questioner eye contact during your response. Quite the opposite. The questioner receives the same amount of eye contact that everybody else gets. The problem is the questioner usually receives twice as much eye contact as everyone else. You'll favor the questioner because he or she asked the question. Don't. Remember, the questioner simply acts as the spokesperson for the group.

Comments versus Questions

In Q&A, you'll need to recognize that a comment is not a question. Seems obvious but it isn't always. For example, during the Q&A someone says, "We're making a big mistake buying this new system." It would be natural to react defensively, but don't. Instead do the opposite. This will take the power out of your opponent's jab. You respond, "Thank you, Butch, I appreciate your comment. (Pause two seconds.) However, our technology team spent days evaluating the need for a new system and found that . . ."

A comment can be positive. "This new system proposal is great! It will solve many of our problems." Don't fumble this pass. Simply respond, "Well, thank you, Ann. I greatly appreciate your support!" Then consider turning to the commenter and saying, "Ann, would you like to add any more thoughts on this proposal?"

Turning over control to the commenter even briefly is a risk, but it might be a risk worth taking if you suspect it will help further validate your pitch.

As you respond with comments, make sure your body language and facial expression are conveying the same message as your words and tone of voice. For instance, consider what happens if you turn and ask, "Butch, would you like to add any more thoughts on this proposal?" Imagine how the meaning would change if you smirked after asking the question and gave a sly look at your colleague who was helping you with the pitch? Or more subtly, what if you asked that question and your body was rigid with tension? Or what if you took an aggressive step toward Butch when you asked it? The bottom line is that you need to be aware of the image you're presenting to people, not just what you're saying. During informal Q&A sessions, you may let down your visual guard. Don't fall into this common trap.

Two-Part Questions

You'll hear, "I have two questions. The first is . . ." Listen to both questions; then pick the one you like best. Put the question you like least on the backburner. When you finish your response to the first question, the second question may not come immediately to mind. If it doesn't, simply ask, "And your second question is?" Frequently even the questioner has forgotten the second one and you can move on. Don't try to juggle two questions and two answers at the same time. Your body language and expression will probably betray this juggling act, making you appear tentative and distracted.

Complimenting the Questioner

Some consultants recommend that you should respond to people with, "I'm glad you asked me that question" or "Excellent question." We strongly disagree. The moment you say to one person,

"Good question," and you don't compliment the next questioner, you risk slighting that person. Besides, if it's a brilliant question, the group will recognize that without your saying so.

Praising some and not others could, in fact, discourage questions. Participants might start thinking, "Maybe I shouldn't ask my question. It might not be excellent or well thought out."

If you want to communicate subtly to one member of a group that a question was a good one, use a subtle visual technique. Nod your head slightly and smile. Lean forward (not step) when answering a particular good question. All these visual responses will get through to the person who asked the good question without offending others.

Jump Starting More Questions

If you think the Q&A is dying after only a few questions, you can revive it. Go back to a transition type question. After a few seconds of silence and no hands go up, you could say, "I'm often asked why . . ." Or, "A question on this topic that frequently comes up is . . ." When you're finished posing and answering your own question, raise your hand and say, "Questions!"

Raising your hand is a visual catalyst. Other visual catalysts might include pointing (open palm), putting your hands in motion when you articulate your transition question or showing a slide again that you used in your pitch and emphasizing the importance of the point the visual was making. This "second sense" input often stimulates people to ask questions that they otherwise would have kept to themselves. It's almost as if they need something besides a verbal cue to get their mouths moving.

The Ideal Q&A

The best Q&A occurs when many people ask questions. For this to happen, sellers need to keep their answers short and then quickly give participants the opportunity for more questions. Keep the pace moving, smile, and use good eye contact to encourage the flow of questions. Don't try to remember the multiple hands that were up. If you can, fine. Otherwise just shoot your hand back up and say, "Questions!"

The Short Form

1. Summarize your pitch . . . pause.
2. End with, "Before I get into questions . . ." followed with one of the three transitions.
3. Finish with only one word, "Questions!"
4. Raise your hand.
5. Move your eyes slowly from one side of the room to the other and back.
6. Pause . . . keep your hand up.
7. Try to start with a friendly questioner.
8. Lower your hand pointing, open palm, to the questioner.
9. Respond, "Yes, question (name)."
10. Questioner receives 100 percent eye contact.
11. Pause two seconds.
12. Move your eyes to the opposite side and farthest listener.
13. Repeat the question in a shorten form.
14. Rephrase the question to at least neutral.
15. Respond with a relatively short answer.
16. Move your eye contact throughout the group in both your repeat and response.
17. Don't favor the questioner with eye contact.
18. Don't end your response on the questioner.
19. To revive or lengthen Q&A, use a transition question.
20. Handle comments/remarks differently than questions.
21. Never step toward the questioner/commenter.
22. Never "go" one to one with the questioner/commenter.
23. Smile often.

One-to-One Q&A

There are two important Q&A group techniques that apply directly to one-on-one selling—pausing and repeating the question. Both techniques help you sell more effectively—and more visually—in response to aggressive questioning.

Pausing

A natural tendency exists to jump in and reply to a question, especially one that challenges your expertise or experience. If the questioner's words head in a negative direction, your itch to respond probably intensifies. You can't wait to correct the misinformation. For instance, imagine that you're an insurance agent for high net worth individuals, and you're closing in on a big deal with a young dot-com billionaire who is interested in purchasing a variety of life insurance and financial plans for himself and his family. And then he asks, "How many policies have you sold to someone in my income bracket?" No doubt, the question makes you feel like he's doubtful about your ability. Your "defensive" response is to list all the clients you've handled who have been wealthy and even add, "A few of them have purchased even larger policies than the one you're contemplating." Even if you don't add that remark, your body language may well betray that this is what you're thinking.

Therefore, use pausing as a technique to resist this impulse. In other words, coach yourself to integrating pausing into all your one-on-one Q&As. Within a pause, concentrate on preventing your eyes from flaring with anger, your mouth from tightening in a grimace, or your body from going tense, as if you're a jungle cat ready to pounce. Don't grip the edge of the table or grind your teeth. These immediate visual responses will work against you from a selling point, communicating your impatience, defensiveness and inability to accept another point of view.

Pausing verbally and visually also allows customers and prospects to complete their thoughts and feel "purged" of whatever objection or idea your pitch evoked. If you pause, you'll probably allow the other person to:

- *Fully vent.* Pausing helps questioners to release their entire bundle of concerns.

- *Reveal the real objection.* In the space between their query and your response, they can arrive at their actual question: "bugs in the program are a big concern! . . . but we need immediate installation. Can you debug as we go after installation?"

- *Ignore the question.* If you pause, questioners may keep right on going and overlook their initial negative question. "Why are your prices so high! . . . You know, people think just because we are a foundation and give away money, they can overcharge us! In fact, the more we spend, the less we have to giveaway. . . . So when we buy, we asked vendors to . . ."

We've found that question-and-answer sessions are especially perilous to making the sale when it's a one-on-one situation. Many prospective buyers may pay polite attention during the formal pitch, but they've been waiting to see how the seller does when he or she no longer is working off a script. The buyer wants to see if this individual can think on his or her feet, how he or she responds to tough questions and so on. Sellers who don't pause generally do make mistakes. They fall into whatever traps a clever buyer sets, and they come across as impulsive and angry rather than thoughtful and calm. Pausing, therefore, provides a way to avoid these negative responses.

Remember, too, that you must pause with both your mouth and your entire body. We've seen salespeople who are able to pause verbally but appear as though they're clenching their mouths so tightly because they don't want any ill-advised words to slip out. We've seen others who don't say anything, but whose eyes are so bright with anger that they might as well tell the prospect what they think of their question. A full body pause, therefore, is the goal.

Repeating the Question

Your brain often needs a second to kick in, especially after feeling the slap of a negative or hostile question. The natural tendency is to immediately pull the trigger and return "enemy fire." Again, one-on-one situations tend to create more anger in the seller than group situations. The social constraints imposed by a group make it easier to use your pause tool. In one on ones, though, you may respond as if you've been slapped. If you find that the pause doesn't work for you, here's a second alternative: repeat the question.

You're at your fifth meeting with the IT purchasing head of a large corporation. You've invested a great deal of time and effort to provide a proposal for the tailored system requested, and you have answered many questions regarding the proposal. You antici-pated clinching the deal during the meeting, and things are going well until you hit the Q&A. The purchasing executive asks you why there's a $500 additional charge for a user manual built into the proposal, saying "I don't get it? We're willing to spend a mil-lion bucks on the system you're proposing, but you're tacking on a $500 charge for a user manual? That seems greedy to me."

"Greedy," you want to respond. "Greedy is what your com-pany's middle name should be, given how much you mark up your services."

All the anger and frustrations that have been building up over the course of your five meetings with this executive threatens to boil over in response to this question. But instead of allowing this to happen, you repeat the question in a positive way, "You're asking me about the extra $500 charge?" Pause, pause. While you're re-peating the question, you're rapidly thinking about the $500 num-ber. It instantly clicks. You now grasp what probably happened. You realize he's not just pushing your buttons but has a legitimate point. After rephrasing his question, you calmly look the ques-tioner in the eye and say, "I agree with you. The charge sounds wrong. But I think I know the answer. I remember that we had this problem before, since the manual is listed as a $500 item, but it's never charged when it's part of a large deal like this one. So I apol-ogize for the coding error and I'll make sure it's eliminated."

When you repeat the question, eye contact is essential. You're communicating that you're not shying away from the tough question but are attempting to answer it honestly and directly.

Whether standing or sitting, don't fidget when you repeat the question. Don't rock back and forth or look away. Don't run your hands through your hair or allow any nervous gesture to surface. Visually, you want to demonstrate that you're giving the repeated question serious consideration. Your stillness and concentration help deliver this message.

Make repeating the question a habit. Then, when the ugly question surfaces, you'll react professionally rather than emotionally. Your "repeat" should take the question to neutral ground and shorten it. First, repeat the question as you neutralize it. "You're asking me about our pricing?" Or, "Your question concerns our pricing?" Second, consider shortening the question. Your repeat could be as short as, "Our cost?" Or "Pricing?" Say either wording slowly. Then you'll still buy yourself enough time to consider the answer.

Let us end this chapter with a brief anecdote: A leader was greatly respected. A new employee asked, "Why is Michelle so well-liked?" The answer: "She always tastes the words before saying them." This is also excellent advice for Q&A.

4

The Big 12
Derailing Details

"God is in the details."

—Mies Van der Rohe, architect

So far, we have emphasized the major problems that result when you literally lose focus—when you fail to keep all eyes on you from the moment you start presenting to the end of the Q&A session. We've found, however, that salespeople are also vulnerable to other visual-related mistakes—mistakes that are diverse and easily overlooked. As you'll discover, these errors often have to do with how the room "looks" or how you're positioned relative to a screen. It is unfortunate how often the million-dollar sales presentation day arrives, the team walks in and they are thrown when they realize they have overlooked a preventable error. Even worse, they lose the sale without understanding the visual mistakes that cost them the deal.

We will examine these 12 oversights and suggest what you can do to stop them from destroying an otherwise effective pitch. We'll also identify slip ups that you may not realize are mistakes. Let's start, though, with the most obvious blunder—not showing up early enough to defeat "Murphy."

Mistake 1: Overlooking "Murphy"

The "Murphy" referred to in this first mistake involves Murphy's Law: If it can go wrong, it will go wrong. Many times, salespeople are very good at checking and double-checking what they're going to say, but not so diligent about what a prospect is going to see. As a result, they are vulnerable to what we call "environmental" mistakes. In other words, presenters walk into the room where they're going to make the pitch and something is wrong. It's often difficult to do a room inspection before the actual presentation because of logistics. Most of the time, however, you have access to a room or you can at least ask someone basic questions about layout and equipment. Problems can be as simple as lighting or as complex as sitting decision makers in the wrong chairs.

The following story serves as a cautionary tale of why every salesperson should anticipate potential Murphys and go the extra mile to take proactive measures.

A company wanted the perfect setting for a multimillion-dollar sales presentation. The team rented an exquisite meeting room at an expensive resort. The sales vice persident requested pictures of the room, asked many important questions, and followed up continuously. All seemed perfect—beautiful resort facilities with an impressive meeting room.

The client and prospect teams fly in late the night before. The sales team checks out the meeting room at 8 A.M. a good hour before the presentation. Everything was laid out just as promised except for one glaring problem. The room overlooked a magnificent large, outdoor swimming pool.

Unfortunately, two days before, the hotel had sent out the room curtains for cleaning. When the hotel set up the room that night, it was dark outside and the night banquet manager knew nothing about the missing curtains nor did anything look amiss. The next morning the sales team knew they faced a terrible presentation environment with string bikinis strutting around the swimming pool that lay not far from the undraped boardroom windows.

The seller should have flown in at least by noon the day before. Then there would have been time to demand that the curtains be retrieved from the cleaners or the meeting be moved to another room or folding screens be rented to block the swimming pool views. Now there was less than an hour until "show" time. With all meeting rooms booked, no other options existed except to go ahead with the room and its distracting view. Needless to say, too many heads turned too often to view the swimmers and not the sellers. The presentation went poorly.

Always allow sufficient time to deal with "Murphy." If possible, visit an important presentation room at least a day in advance. If that's not possible, ask someone to take pictures of it with a digital camera from different angles and e-mail you the photos. You might also want to ask the client or prospect a few questions about the room—its technical capabilities, the light levels, the size, if there are any distracting elements—so you know what you're in for and can either prepare or seek other options.

Mistake 2: Delivering Split Presentations

It is difficult to read the subtitles of a foreign movie and follow the action. As viewers focus on the text, they inevitably miss part of the drama. When sellers stand at a distance from the screen, they create a similar problem (Figure 4.1).

The seller and screen are two distinct messages. The former involves the presenter's words, tone of voice and appearance—clothes, jewelry, facial expressions, gestures, and leg or arm movements. The latter is the screen visuals.

When too much space exists between the seller and screen, people cannot see and absorb both at the same time. Their attention shifts back and forth, as if they were watching a tennis match.

Figure 4.1 Split Presentation

Viewers look from the screen, to the presenter gesturing, back to the screen and the next visual, then to the seller who makes an emphatic point, and then back to a new slide. At any given moment, when the speaker and screen are apart, viewers are forced to choose between competing focal points.

There is no need to create this conflict. To avoid a split presentation, stand right next to the screen, flipchart, or chart board. Viewers then see and process you and your visuals as one message rather than two. You should also reinforce this "togetherness" by pointing and working with the images. Be "one" with the visual.

When you sell one on one from a laptop, you also split your presentation. The person who is next to you or on the other side of the desk must constantly choose whether to look at the laptop screen or switch to you when you, emphasize key points. Your prospect cannot focus on both you and your laptop simultaneously (Figure 4.2).

You probably won't build rapport with someone whose focus is repeatedly divided. Without this rapport, you struggle to gauge the prospect's acceptance of your points. Even worse, the more enthusiastic you become, the more often your prospect or customer turns away from the screen to follow your conversation.

Figure 4.2 Laptop Split Presentations

To counteract laptop split presentations, frequent and strategic pausing is critical. When you talk, do not change the screen image. When you click and point, be quiet. Allow listeners to concentrate on you or the screen. Point to the screen after you talk to redirect their attention. Be aware, however, that a certain level of split presentation always exists when you use a laptop. At best, you can moderate the negative impact, but you are never going to be able to eliminate it entirely.

Mistake 3: Positioning Yourself Incorrectly

Right-handed sellers usually stand with the screen to their right. This allows them to point more easily (Figure 4.3). However, people read left to right. Salespeople are unable to capitalize on this fact when the screen is to their right.

Figure 4.3 Standing, Wrong Side

Figure 4.4 Standing Correctly

Stand with the screen to your left (Figure 4.4). Then people will naturally start with their eyes on you and return to you after glancing at the screen. This position also places you in the most "looked at" spot—the left or beginning point, where you start to read sentences.

Mistake 4: Choosing the Wrong Screen Size and Position

In most meeting rooms, screens are two to three times bigger than necessary. Imagine a huge screen, a seller, and five prospects. The bigger the screen, the more it overshadows the presenter (Figure 4.5).

Figure 4.5 Screen Diminishes Presenter

For 2 to 15 people, use a portable 4-foot-by-4-foot screen. If you are stuck with an oversized screen, you do not need to fill it completely. Before you present, sit in a chair in the back row. Enlarge the screen image only enough to see it comfortably from your back-row chair.

Recessed ceiling screens are typically centered. This provides nice room symmetry, but it also diminishes the seller. With a large, centered screen, the presenter stands to the side, and the screen becomes the focal point (Figure 4.6).

Increase your chance to sell your ideas effectively with a portable screen. Place yourself in the room's center or key spot, and then angle the screen about 25 degrees toward yourself. A slanted screen to the side positions the seller as the focal point—the essence of visual selling.

Figure 4.6 Screen Wrongly in Center

Mistake 5: Seating Decision Makers in the Wrong Chairs

In important sales presentations, seating arrangements matter. The first chair to the presenter's left (A) is the best viewing point for a decision maker and chair (E) the least desirable (Figure 4.7).

The rationale for this seating arrangement is that even a good presenter will mistakenly favor the screen and turn leftward. Therefore, plant your feet firmly perpendicular to your group and be conscious that your body will continuously try to rotate toward the screen. Because the screen exerts this leftward pull, you will also mistakenly give more eye contact to (A) and (B) than (E) and (D).

Mistake 6: Dimming the Lights

Darkness induces drowsiness and mental wandering (Figure 4.8). Keep the room lights on or dim them slightly. The seller should be

Figure 4.7 Table Seating, with Presenter and Screen

Figure 4.8 Dark Rooms Induce Sleep

visible. Darkness eliminates the best part of a presentation—you. A presenter may feel less nervous hiding in the darkness and letting the screen dominate, but it is bad strategy. A dark room suggests the screen's message is more important than you. As a seller, you are there to add meaning, emphasis, and motivation. Without you, the pitch might as well be emailed to your prospect's computer.

If multiple light switches are available, turn off the lights directly above the screen or unscrew bulbs over it. If you must choose between having all the lights on or all off, keep them on. As an American Indian proverb goes, "Move closer to the campfire so I can see your words." With the lights on, you will be seen, heard, and more likely believed.

Since the lights are on, you will need to design slides that are visible at higher light levels. For this situation, graphic designers can recommend a background color to make the slide content clear and readable.

Mistake 7: Promoting the Screen

Let's say that in your spare time you are an avid a mountain climber or art expert. You often give slide presentations on your passion to expand your network of contacts. You might think that it's the picture (slide) of the difficult climb or stunning work of art that deserves the attention—not the speaker. Therefore, doesn't it make sense to darken the room so the mountain or art is presented in all its glory?

While the audience attends the talk to see the peaks or the paintings, they also need to see the speaker. As the audience listens to the climber's daring skill or the curator's insightful knowledge, people also want to "see" the face of courage, endurance, or research and interpretation.

Many stunning books show rugged mountain views and exquisite art objects. Your presence pulls an audience into the challenge of the climb or the beauty of the art. If you darken the room and use only the podium light, you appear insignificant. You are there to make the slides come alive, to make them more than just photos in an art book. You, as well as the slides, are the show.

Mistake 8: Playing with Pointers and other Toys

Do not use mechanical or laser pointers, and do not hold pencils, pens, or markers in your hands. They become playthings with which you'll fidget. You might as well twirl a baton, since your hands gripping some object will distract people just as much. If you need to channel nervous energy, point and gesture rather than wave an object.

Your left arm is the best pointer. You won't twirl it, push it in, pull it out, cap or uncap it, drop it, jab yourself with it, or become an orchestra leader (Figure 4.9).

Laser pointers encourage you to wander away from the screen. You force viewers to choose between watching you or the visual and its jumping laser beam (Figure 4.10). When you stand next to the screen and point with your left arm, you won't create a split presentation. Unless you are speaking to a ballroom of a thousand faces, get rid of pointers, especially laser ones; they often lead to embarrassing faux pas.

For example, a senior vice president was reviewing the annual sales numbers in a darkened hotel ballroom at a large meeting of a company's sales and marketing executives. His slides dripped with

Figure 4.9 Orchestra Leader

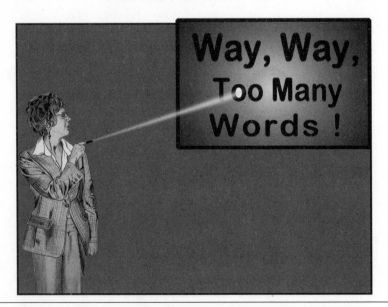

Figure 4.10 Laser Pointers Encourage Split Presentations

way too many figures. As he tediously plowed through the numbers, he suddenly saw that with a backward step, his laser pointer circle grew bigger. He realized that the figures he just covered could now be included with the next number he planned to discuss. Once he processed this brilliant insight, it took him just four backward moves to fall off the raised ballroom platform. Only the announcement that the presenter had broken an arm and there would be an intermission quieted the waves of laughter.

Mistake 9: Blocking the Screen

Do not turn into the visual and point with your right arm. This causes you to partially block the screen from viewers to your right. Instead, point only with your left arm and hand. An open

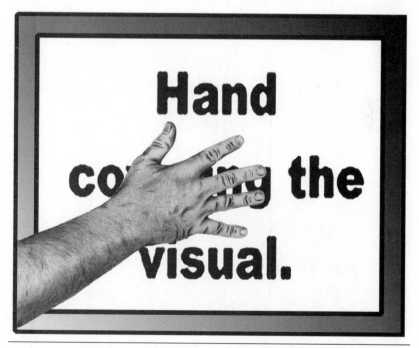

Figure 4.11 Hands Covering the Visual

palm, flat against the screen might cause you to cover up the very item you wish to highlight (Figure 4.11 on previous page). Instead, keep your palm down and parallel to the floor with your fingers together. Use a slow, clean karate chop movement to underscore your image.

Mistake 10: Holding Remotes and Clickers

Do not hold the remote or clicker (Figure 4.12). It's human nature to play with objects in your hands. If you're nervous, you'll speed up and change the slides faster than you should. Besides, holding a remote causes you to gesture less. You'll settle into the easier, boring role of a talking head instead of selling your ideas with your upper body.

Figure 4.12 Do Not Hold the Remote

In addition, avoid having someone else work the remote or laptop. Your signals can easily be crossed, producing embarrassing timing mistakes. No doubt, you've seen presentations where the slide-changer and presenter were out of synch, reminiscent of a badly dubbed foreign film where the speaker's words lag behind his mouth movements. You control your content, and only you should change the slides.

You should never speak while you're doing something physical—clicking to the next slide, turning chart paper or mounting a chart board. People will process a visual *before* they shift and take in your spoken words. If you speak, they will hear little of what you say. Let your audience quench their visual curiosity before you talk. Allow a two- to three-second pause while you make the change and viewers soak up the visual.

Mistake 11: Positioning the Lectern to the Side

Usually, in high-dollar sales presentations two items, beside the presenter, dominate the room—the screen and lectern. Most presenters seriously confuse the relationship of these two items and their use. Presenters place the lectern well away from the screen and then they hide behind the "box." To "take cover" defeats the whole idea of selling visually. In Chapter 10, we'll talk about how to deliver to the side of a lectern and project the image of an expert. For mistake number 11, we'll simply touch on the lectern's correct position.

The seller stands center stage, with the angled screen to his or her immediate left. A lectern that holds your laptop, remote, or notes is positioned one step to the right. You should present standing between the lectern and the screen (Figure 4.13). Or you can place the remote on a small table that fits under the screen. The second or two it takes you to step over to change the slide, forces you to slow down and pause.

Position the lectern, screen, and presenter together so the presenter can interact closely with the screen and use the nearby

Figure 4.13 Lectern to the Side

lectern to hold content cue cards or the remote to change slides. Separating the screen from the lectern and speaker immediately splits the message and weakens the presentation.

Mistake 12: Reading Someone Else's Text Slides

Let's say your sales teammate, who created the text slides, calls in sick. At the last minute, your boss makes you the lead sales person (or it may be that your partner, who was going to lead the pitch, falls sick and you are pressed into action). The problem, of course, is that you're stuck with a text-heavy pitch that lacks visual sales appeal.

Even though the text slides will cripple you, arrange the room to your advantage: an angled, portable screen, no split presentation or pointers. Turn the lights on. And most important, keep the decks or handouts out of sight until you're finished.

When you present, be very enthusiastic. That helps viewers overlook the boring slides. As each bullet-point list lights up the screen, don't read it. Summarize key items with different words. For example, assume you're delivering the numbing text slide shown in Figure 4.14.

To make a text slide a bit more palatable, always pause three full seconds as the list hits the screen or you reveal a line. This gives listeners a quick, quiet moment to read. And, you can bet they will!

Then say:

I want to introduce four key projects we in the Jelly Bean Division hope to accomplish next year. First, I will address the new incentive plan (pointing to retain more key . . .), then how we'll strengthen consumer interest (pointing to build stronger brand . . .), keep the owners happy, and last, lower manufacturing costs. Now let me get into the details on the first item and most important (pointing again to key employees), how we'll energize bright people like you!

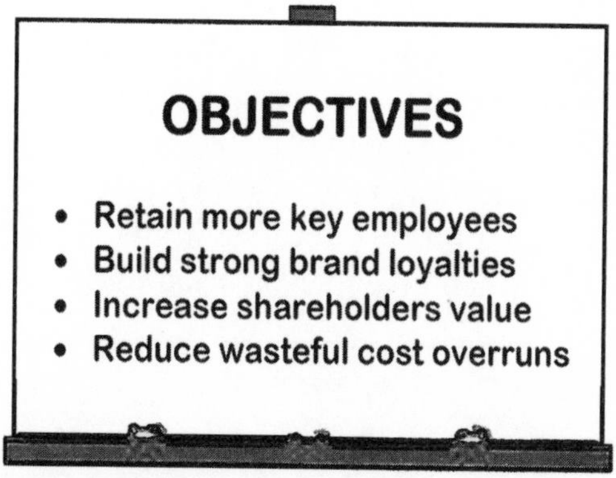

OBJECTIVES

- Retain more key employees
- Build strong brand loyalties
- Increase shareholders value
- Reduce wasteful cost overruns

Figure 4.14 Objectives Text Slide

Keep your enthusiasm level high and don't read *any* words from the screen. Then maybe, at least, half the group will be awake when you finish.

Little Mistakes Can Become Big Errors

It may be that these 12 visual mistakes seem relatively minor. How important is it really, if you hold a pen in your hand as you talk or if you are standing on the wrong side of the screen? If you do a good job of positioning the product or service, you're selling and connecting with a prospect or customer, isn't everything else secondary? Not necessarily. As you well know, prospects often have to make choices between products or services where there is relatively little differentiation. The pricing and features are similar, and customers find that the competing salespeople are intelligent and trustworthy. The deciding factor is often an individual's "sense" of the salesperson. It's not always something he or she can put into words, but it's just that one seller seems better than another does.

Many times, this sense is a direct result of something visual. Make a number of the visual mistakes described here and prospects won't feel comfortable with you. Block the screen and people will miss a crucial element of your presentation. Place a key decision maker in the wrong seat in the room and you miss the opportunity to make consistent eye contact with this individual. However, if you avoid these mistakes, you will present a much better image both literally and figuratively.

Finally, don't feel as if these mistakes are inevitable. They all are preventable with a bit of forethought and planning. Here are 12 positive steps you can take to avoid each of the 12 mistakes:

The Short Form

1. Show up at least half-a-day early to battle "Murphy."
2. Stand next to the screen and present a united message.

---

3. Position a screen, flip chart, or easel stand to your left.
4. Choose the right screen size for the group and angle it.
5. Place your key viewers where they will best see you.
6. Keep the lights at their highest brightness so people stay alert and see you.
7. Promote your presence, not just the screen.
8. Keep your hands free to gesture by not holding a pointer, marker, or remote.
9. Point at the screen with your fingers together, palm down and parallel to the floor. Point to the screen with only your left arm, but when you gesture, use both arms.
10. Place your laptop or remote on the lectern or on a table under the screen.
11. Stand in the center of the room or stage with the screen to the left and lectern to the right.
12. Use different words than what appears on the screen if circumstances force you to use someone else's text slides.

5

Eliminating Decks and Delaying Handouts

You're great at avoiding the previous chapter's 12 mistakes. You may also have established a good visual presence and command buyers' attention. Now you must be careful not to negate this presence by misusing decks and handouts, subjects we touched on in the first chapter.

Unfortunately, salespeople often labor under the mistaken notion that they must prepare people for the "sell" with advance material. Presenters believe that if they hand out hard copies of their slides upfront, they will pack more into their pitch and viewers will absorb the information better. This is a classic visual mistake. Let's look how it's made and how to avoid it.

Visual Competition

Imagine you are about to propose marriage to someone with whom you are madly in love. In your mind, you have researched what you want to say, and you know you can make a compelling argument to convince her to say yes. You get down on bended knee and you begin your proposal. But first, you provide her with a written summary of your main points.

This obviously would be ludicrous. You would draw her attention away from you eloquently emoting on bended knee and direct it toward the handout. In addition, no matter how moving or mesmerizing the rest of your proposal might be, she is going to be spending a lot of it staring at the piece of paper you gave her. After all, it's human nature. We learn from early schooling to read the materials the teacher gave us. Many times in class, teachers would have us follow a lecture by referring to mimeographed sheets of paper or refer to pages in a book open on our desks.

Most of us would not propose marriage with a handout. However, many commit this sin when trying to make a sale. Some salespeople may keep their handouts out of sight when they're selling one to one, but as soon as two or more prospects gather in a room, they fall back into grade school teacher mode and start passing things out.

Some consultants claim presenters should not try to control group behavior. While you may not be able to control certain factors—whether a prospect is sleepy, poor lighting in a customer's conference room—you can and *should* control the room visually. After spending a considerable amount of time organizing and practicing your presentation, you should do everything possible to focus your group on what you are saying and showing.

Admittedly, this can be a challenge. Even sellers with excellent delivery skills must work hard to hold a group's attention. People are easily distracted by anyone entering or leaving the meeting or loud conversation in the hallway. If, at the beginning of your pitch, you are foolish enough to distribute a document, you are just adding to the sensory clutter. You just gave prospects or customers a legitimate reason not to pay attention to you or the screen.

To avoid distracting prospects, delay handouts, and eliminate decks. People often keep either as a file copy and those who could not attend read it to learn what they missed. Handouts that viewers receive afterwards are fine, but anything distributed before or during your pitch will draw prospective buyers' eyes and minds away from you or the screen. When they are thumbing through a deck while you sell your ideas, it is as if two people are talking simultaneously. Decks often provide the louder voice, in that they encourage people to treasure hunt.

Decks offer the possibility of hidden gems. Early in the presentation, your prospects and customers will leaf through the deck to find these treasures, convinced that it, rather than you, contains the key details that will help them make a buying decision. The more questions your presentation raises, the more likely that your group will seek the answers in the deck. For example, people may be thinking "Is volume pricing offered?" Or "How will this new proposed system affect in-house jobs?" Or "What's the bottom line, the recommendations proposed?" As prospects scour the deck for answers, they completely ignore you and the screen.

This unfortunate event takes place even when you're selling one on one. You may assume that in this situation, no one would be so rude as to look at the written materials you've given him or her. In fact, your prospect may feel it is rude not to look at them. After all, you put this large package of words together. Should he or she just ignore it? When you're selling directly to one individual, you don't want even the thinnest piece of paper to stand between you and the sale. Don't give this prospect a visual alternative to you.

Good sellers try hard to develop a persuasive sequence. As people absorb deck pages, however, they are not fully concentrating on your logic that indicates conviction or sincerity. They also miss most of your facial expressions and vocal inflections. Consequently, as prospects dig through your document for answers to questions you have raised or more substantive detail on points you have made, you end up presenting to yourself. You can't motivate them to buy if they don't pay attention.

Clear the Decks: Dealing with People's Expectations

Let's say you are ready to start your presentation and someone asks, "Hey, where's the deck?" To manage this problem gracefully, consider leaving the documents in your office or car. Then you can honestly reply, "I'm very sorry. I was in a terrific hurry and accidentally left them in my car; but I intend, right now, to summarize for you all the key points in a short overview and immediately after the presentation distribute them though e-mail or interoffice mail. Stay with me. I promise to give it my best and not disappoint you with this 'deckless' presentation."

You may also find yourself in a situation where your "I left them in the car" excuse will not suffice. You may be presenting to a group that not only expects a desk but also insists on it. Your contact may tell you, "The boss loves to follow along with decks, so you absolutely need to hand out something." In these instances, print full-page versions of your image slides and duplicate them to create your deck. This is an acceptable compromise. With an "image-deck," your audience will not be overly distracted.

In fact, you'll quickly see the big difference between listeners studying a "text-deck" versus an "image-deck." With a text driven deck, heads are down and the eyes glued to the copy. With "images decks," people rapidly peruse the entire deck and return their attention to you. The viewer's "fast take" occurs because image pages only broadly indicate where the seller is heading. It gives the skeleton of your message, but it doesn't flesh it out in a way that is absorbing. Images need a presenter to fill in the details. As a result, your viewers will listen that much harder while you speak.

You may feel that you must have a stand-alone handout for a key person who wants to be informed but can't attend. Or you may need a record of the presentation for legal reasons, or as a file copy. Perhaps most commonly, you want prospects and customers to have a more comprehensive take-away than just pages of images.

If you need both an image deck and a substantive handout, make them separate. The deck—if you must distribute a document before you start—should contain $8\frac{1}{2} \times 11$ copies of your image slides (Figure 5.1). The handout, which you distribute afterward, should have pages combining your image slides and related text. The handout becomes a stand-alone document. Using the PowerPoint notes pane, the handout page might look like Figure 5.2—one-third image, two-thirds text.

Figure 5.1 Image Slide for Image Deck

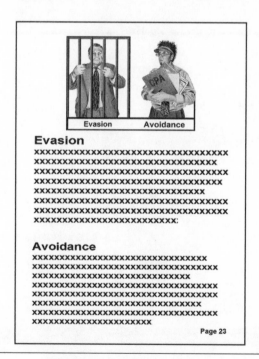

Figure 5.2 Handout Page

In certain circumstances such as a highly technical training presentation, you might need to pass out a skeleton deck before you speak. For example, as a seasoned financial analyst, your indirect sales presentation shows commercial loan officers how to spot risky companies. The half-day presentation covers complex terms and some math formulas.

You want to use images to simplify the technical concepts and add enjoyment to your presentation. The first image you scan into a slide looks like Figure 5.3.

You project the "Highly-Leveraged" slide on the screen and say, "Let me discuss the first warning sign of credit problems." Then you pass out a skeleton page (Figure 5.4) and say, "Here's a copy of this slide with extra space, if you're a jotter." This treats participants as adults. They decide whether to take notes or listen.

Figure 5.3 Highly Leveraged

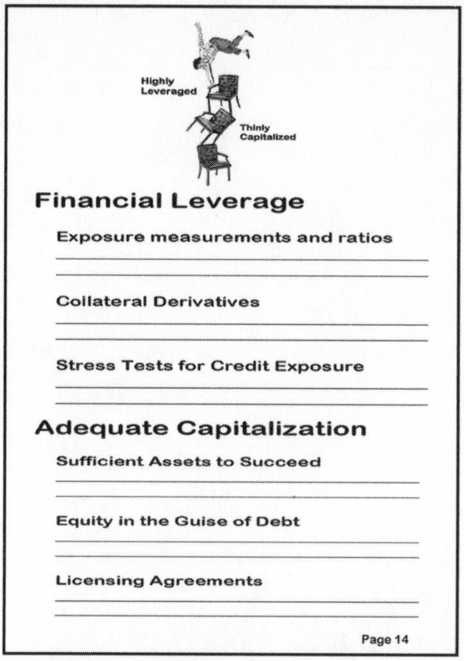

Figure 5.4 Skeleton Deck Page

In the notes section of the slide, you list only major points that support your image. Print out your slideshow in the notes format, with the image on the top fourth or fifth of the page and the key points with blank lines below.

To promote active listening, the skeleton deck page should contain only headlines or key phrases, not sentences. Because the skeleton deck pages do not spell out the details, your listeners won't read while you speak. They can selectively add notes or simply listen to you—their choice. At the end of your presentation, pass out a second, filled in version as a handout. This reinforces your message and provides a valuable, stand-alone reference.

Yes, two documents require much more work, but outstanding results require outstanding preparation. It takes extra time and effort to be an ace seller of ideas.

6

Images: The Perfect Selling Partner

Books about the art of persuasion often cite the following quote from the Greek classics: When Pericles spoke, people said, "How well he speaks," but when Demosthenes spoke, they said, "Let us march."

If you possess great delivery skills like Demosthenes, you don't need much else. When you ask people to march off to war or redirect their lives, visual extras like PowerPoint slides would likely diminish the impact of your message. Many motivational speakers, too, rely only on a dynamic presentation and don't use props.

Also, in rare instances, content is so powerful that it makes extra visuals unnecessary. Lincoln at Gettysburg or Roosevelt's words on the Japanese attack at Pearl Harbor are examples of talks that are moving because of Lincoln's speechwriting skills or Roosevelt's momentous message. They didn't need visuals.

Most of us aren't great speechwriters and we don't have news with world-changing content. Often, we are well aware of our shortcomings as presenters. We want the extra visual support.

Therefore, we darken the room, stand off to the side, drench the screen with text, and annoy listeners by reading to them. We use word slides to prop us up, but in fact, they are knocking us down.

In contrast to word slides, image slides can increase the persuasiveness of your sales pitch in many ways. Using images as visual props, you'll see how they trump text slides in almost every sales situation. Let's consider why researchers have concluded that images deliver incredibly memorable, convincing sales messages.

The Case for Image Visuals

Most advertising contains an image of some sort, from a simple logo to an elaborate series of graphics. While advertisers may have a great deal to say about their products and services, they recognize that a tremendous amount of clutter exits in various advertising media. As a result, they rely heavily on images to communicate their message fast, memorably, and persuasively. This reliance isn't just based on their "gut." A great deal of research has been done about why advertising sells.

Images Increase Credibility

Paul Messaris (1997), in his book *Visual Persuasion*, has investigated what makes images work. He finds that some images, like photos, offers "proof" that something exists. Most people look at a photo of footprints in the sand and assume that someone walked down the shore. By the same logic, we unconsciously believe photos in ads. For example, car ads often show an SUV on a high mountain ridge or peak (Figure 6.1). Most viewers, if questioned, would say, "Well, yes, I understand that the vehicle couldn't have been driven there." However, that doesn't matter. What's important and implied is that "This is one tough vehicle because it can climb rugged terrain." Forget that a helicopter "steered" it to the top. The picture offers "proof" of toughness, regardless of how the vehicle got there.

Figure 6.1 SUV on Top

You can talk all you want about customer service, guarantees, and price points, but if you really want to convince a prospect that your words are credible, you'll send a reinforcing message through images. It may be as simple as a logo that backs up your claim that your company is solid, like the insurance company that has a logo of a huge rock. You might include some candid photos of your people at work to validate your claim that they're friendly, hard-working, and accessible. Whether you use an image as a symbol or as a literal representation of a selling point, you enhance your credibility.

Images Increase Retention

Images aid retention. Most sellers don't hit a home run on every first pitch. Listeners hear them out. Sellers leave and plan for another visit, while prospects might or might not think about what the seller said. If an idea is to be considered, it must be remembered. The longer and stronger the idea lingers, the better the chance for a "yes" decision. Therefore, the question is: Are image messages more memorable than communications that are spoken or read?

The mind stores and retrieves pictures more efficiently than words. A face is easier to remember and recall than a name. Cognitive psychologists call this phenomenon the "picture superiority effect." Pictures are easier to recall than words, in both the short term and the long term (Higbee, 2001, pp. 64–78). In one study, subjects recognized 612 pictures with 98 percent accuracy in the short term and even recognized 58 percent of them after 120 days (Shepard, 1967).

When it comes to retention, think about your own experiences. You go to a neighborhood picnic. You meet dozens of people but spend most of your time talking to about five partygoers. A month later, you bump into one of the five. Instantly you recognize his or her face, but, of course, you have forgotten the name. Remembering faces over names happens all the time.

Think about a password you use only once a month. You remember it for six straight months, and then suddenly you can't recall it. On the other hand, 20 years later, would you have trouble visualizing your teenage sweetheart or even your closest high school friends? Probably not. Pictures stick for a long time—often for a lifetime. That makes images an invaluable, subconscious selling partner.

Consider retention from a prospect's standpoint. In highly competitive situations, the prospect may have met with three, four, or more different sellers. Invariably, the message each seller sends fades with time. They may all run together, and one seller's message is confused with another's. If you have incorporated a powerful image into your presentation, however, that prospect will recall it much longer than he or she will recall all the words you used in making your pitch. They'll remember that you showed a photo of your product being used in the hinterlands of India or that you repeatedly used a cartoon-like illustration to make a humorous point about your customer service capabilities. Images like these are far "stickier" than words in conversation or word slides alone.

Images Cover More Ground

Have you ever wondered how, in 90 minutes, a movie can tell the same story as a book that took you many hours to read? The opening film scene might show cowboys working a corral filled with restless stallions. Behind the horses sits a large ranch house nestled at the base of spectacular snow-covered mountains. This opening scene in the novel might run five pages. Yet, in the movie, a viewer spends a few seconds taking all this in.

Or think of a resort photo showing an inviting water scene— white sands covering a crescent-shaped beach, lined with palm trees, rolling, gentle waves, shade umbrellas, and thick-cushioned lounge chairs (Figure 6.2).

Figure 6.2 Beach Scene

The description could continue for many more sentences. It might take you maybe 30 to 40 seconds, as you read it, before a full image of that scene would form in your mind. But with a photograph or illustration, you "get it" instantly. That's a huge advantage for images.

This "quick take" happens for an obvious reason. You might recognize a beach at a glance, while to read about it requires words like sun, sand, palm trees, waves, and surf. The mind processes an image in a single glance.

Words quickly overload our short-term memory. George Miller's (1956) classic study, "The Magic Number Seven, Plus or Minus Two," concludes that short-term memory can hold about seven stimulus inputs at once. Words may be grouped or "chunked" differently from images (Sinatra, 1986).

With words, chunks are no more than the brief pause the eye makes after reading a word or two. With an image, however, the eye takes in the entire concept in one chunk. That's why it takes a viewer 10, 50, 100 times longer to grasp text than the same information shown as an image.

Now consider an image versus words in a business context (Figure 6.3).

Here is the same graphic described in words: Imagine a bar chart containing six columns. The columns are labeled from left to right, A, B, C, D, E, F. The fourth column from the left, D, shows the greatest increase. The first column, A is shorter then E but taller than C. Column B is . . .

Which is easier and quicker to grasp, the image or the words?

Some salespeople, however, feel compelled to explain what their prospects immediately see. They are operating on the misconception that their verbal eloquence trumps the visual. When your goal is to communicate data like statistics, trends, comparative studies, you want to do so with the greatest speed and impact possible.

Salespeople often state and restate a powerful set of statistics, watering down the message by pounding it home five different ways over three or four minutes. By the end of their discussion,

Figure 6.3 Chart with Multiple Columns

prospects have become bored and the message that was originally thought provoking now seems mundane. The simple graphic, however, accomplishes the salesperson's goal in a flash. Salespeople must push their egos aside and recognize that at certain times and in certain situations, a visual is more eloquent than they are, no matter how verbally adept they might be.

Images Stir Emotions

Paul Messaris also notes that images are icons, referring to something familiar. As such, they may elicit an emotional response because of associations with a particular object.

Well-chosen images can leave an emotional impression that is indelible. Think of the photograph showing the sailor in Times Square celebrating the end of World War II by kissing the willing, young woman. Or the Vietnam War photo that captures the exact moment a Vietnamese policeman fired his pistol into the head of his victim. These images immediately seize your attention and elicit an emotional reaction.

Not-for-profit organizations often use images to raise money for relief efforts. The emotional impact of seeing a rail-thin child with her rib bones sticking out is compelling (Figure 6.4). This kind of image pulls you in, stirs strong feelings, and then causes you to respond positively—send a contribution, write a letter, buy a product, or change your behavior.

Remember, though, that if these images are viewed as crass or manipulative, they lose their selling power. It is only when the images feel true and appropriate that they achieve their selling objectives.

Consider how images can use emotion to change behaviors in ways that a few words can't. A company has experienced a string of accidents involving severed fingers because workers were blatantly disregarding cutting machinery safety rules. Warnings, even suspensions, didn't prevent their careless behaviors. Finally, an em-

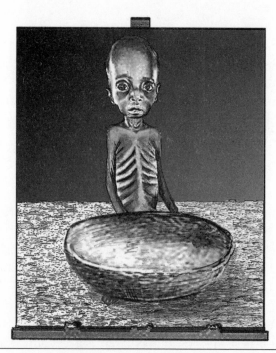

Figure 6.4 Starving Child

ployee suggested placing large photo blowups of bloody hands in the area where the accidents were occurring. Bingo. No more tragedies. The grim photos of mangled palms and mutilated fingers immediately changed workers' behaviors and attitudes.

Insurance marketers frequently rely on emotionally laden images—a family standing outside of a home devastated by flood or fire, for example—to make their messages memorable and motivating. Greeting card companies choose warm and fuzzy images—grandpa playing catch with his grandson—to help sell their product. These images can use everything from sadness to joy to raise money, motivate employees, sell products and services, or encourage investors.

Images Seize Your Attention

To sell, you need to hold viewer attention from the first slide to the last words. Using additional changing stimuli like PowerPoint slides increases activity in the front of the room and draws the eye. Then, because images are unique and offer more visual variety than text, they unconsciously draw more attention. Furthermore, well-designed images almost guarantee continuous attention from prospects and customers. Attention-getting images come in all shapes and sizes, and they may even seem strange or incomprehensible at first glance and still seize people's attention (Messaris, 1997).

Consider the surrealistic art in Figure 6.5. The distorted elements draw you to an art object because they are abnormal. Then the work pulls you in further as you try to make sense of the images. Or perhaps you are drawn to a visual because it's bizarre. You may also have seen ads showing a beautiful, naked woman with a large snake coiled about her, covering her discreetly. Strange images can be strangely mesmerizing.

Messaris tells us that the mind processes information in relationship to what it already knows. When the mind finds no reference point, it attempts to "square" the information. This disconnect benefits the seller. When people attempt to understand an image's meaning, they concentrate deeply on the visual.

Figure 6.5 Surrealistic Art

As a result, their attention is even more intense than if they immediately "got" it. Of course, this doesn't mean you want all your images to be obscure or surreal. If viewers have to struggle too much, they'll give up or lose interest. In general, the point is that an unusual or strange image can have a strong pull. You may show before and after slides of an elephant sitting on your product to demonstrate its durability; you may create an image of your sales staff superimposed over a picture of the North Pole to communicate that your people will go to the ends of the earth to provide good customer service. Sometimes, you face prospects who are bored or jaded and you need something that shakes them out of their torpor and makes them focus on what you're selling. An unusual or even a bizarre image can achieve this effect.

Images Imply What Words Can't

Messaris (1997) also observes that images lack what he refers to as "syntax." In other words, they aren't burdened by the requirements of verbal logic, grammar, specificity, and so on. They allow viewers to supply their own meanings. Thus, we see a plane taking off into the sunset, and we can dream of going on whatever vacation fits our fantasy. Telling people about where this plane is going, however, will rob the individual of his or her own interpretation of it.

Images can make claims or connections that might be unacceptable in words and would never make it through the legal department. However, they can strongly, subconsciously support your point. Sometimes, this "proof" in the sense used by Messaris is manufactured in a prospect's mind. A travel brochure features scenes from the Caribbean Islands, and the individual sitting in a travel agent's office perusing the brochure might recall her own enjoyable cruise to that area. These personal connections make the brochure more powerful, memorable, and persuasive. In a very real way, images can provide the proof that lets customers sell themselves.

Pick up a glossy brochure created by any large, national firm that manages mutual funds. You will find a photo of couples sailing on sleek yachts; sightseeing in exotic, foreign countries; or lying on the beach of luxurious resorts. What's implied is that if you let that fund company manage your portfolio, you'll have money to buy a yacht, fly overseas, or vacation at four-star resorts. However, nowhere in the brochure copy will it state, "we will increase your investment." Marketers or money managers cannot legally put such statements in writing.

A picture, though, can make the vague but compelling promise of an affluent future. An illustration or photograph can suggest you'll make money, even though the text can't. This gives images a *huge* advantage over words, and not just when you are legally prohibited from saying certain things. Not all the verbiage in the world can equal the image or photo of a beautiful aurora borealis or alpenglow. No matter how vividly you write about it, the stunning, multifaceted colors of the scene itself does a better job of making you want to see it in person.

Similarly, you can promise your prospects all sorts of wonderful results if they buy from you, but your words invite a cynical or skeptical reaction. If, on the other hand, you create an image that promises these wonderful results, they are far less likely to be cynical or skeptical. The image helps them form their own ideas, as opposed to having your words imposed on them.

This is not wrong or immoral unless the seller knows with certainty that the image presents a false or misleading picture. Few invest money without thinking they'll increase the value of their portfolio, and the image of a couple on the beach allows people to create a cause-and-effect scenario in their minds: If I invest in Mutual Fund A, I'll be able to afford a fabulous vacation. People recognize the image offers a possibility, not a certainty. But it's the possibility that is an important motivator.

Peruse any luxury resort brochure. The beach photos always show great weather—full sun and inviting waters. These images imply that your vacation will be filled with joyous golfing, swimming, or sailing days. Yet, hurricanes, cloudy days, or beach closings for jellyfish or shark sightings occur. Images allow you to picture the vacation of your dreams, which it may well turn out to be. However, someone selling this paradise in words would sound ridiculous if the writer said that every day of every year is perfect.

Take one last example: toothpaste ads. They show a handsome man and a beautiful woman, each with a bright smile and white teeth. The subtext of this message is that if you brush with this product, you'll possess gleaming teeth and attract the opposite sex. But the copy neither guarantees nor addresses how soon your teeth will look like the model's perfect bicuspids and molars.

Images can imply what you can't or don't want to put into words.

The Short Form

1. Images increase credibility.
2. Images increase retention.
3. Images cover more ground.

4. Images stir emotions.
5. Images seize attention.
6. Images imply what words can't.

Experiential Arguments for Image Visuals

Some of you may be nodding in agreement, while thinking, "Yes, the research makes a strong case for images being powerful but they're not appropriate for my particular selling situation." In fact, it's not that images are inappropriate but just that you haven't found the ones that are well suited to what you're selling.

Images can be used to delivery your entire message. They can help prospects and customers imagine superior results; some can be used as comic relief during a tense pitch; others can help spice up a dry presentation. The possible uses are endless.

Perhaps the most common complaint about images that we hear is, "They aren't appropriate for the seriousness of our business." You should be aware from this research that images are far from frivolous; in fact, they contain powerful psychological, emotional, and informational messages. Even the most innocuous image may contain more meaning than meets the eye. As you've learned, images can make a sales message more memorable and more impactful—both serious business goals.

More specifically, our long years of experience shows that presentations with images usually trounce the competition for two reasons: your credibility and your charisma.

Seller Credibility

We "buy" the seller as much as the product or service. We buy the seller's integrity that the product is well built. We buy the seller's word that he or she will deliver prompt service if it's needed. In short, we buy the seller's confidence and conviction that this is the right product or service for us. Without this assurance, this credibility, few prospects will buy.

Even during in-house presentations—a CEO attempting to convince his top executives of the rightness of his strategy, for instance—people look for a similar commitment. The presenter's abilities comes into consideration as much as the idea that is being promoted.

People wonder, "Do presenters have the determination to carry out the idea they are pushing?" People evaluate salespeople and any presenter from the moment they start to speak. It begins very superficially—the face, body features, what the clothes "say." Then the group drills deeper. What level of honesty, sincerity, and determination does the presenter communicate?

Contrary to popular belief, it is often the intangibles rather than the tangibles that make a sale. In other words, people often sell under the assumption that the merit of their product or service will win an account. People who present to venture capitalists, for instance, often assume that their brilliant business ideas will secure funding. In reality, venture capital firms make decisions about funding based on an individual's credibility, their ability to deliver on what they propose.

Without question, substance is important in selling. Many times, however, competing salespeople are offering similar products and services. In these situations, a buying decision often boils down to how a prospect "feels" about the seller.

It's not easy for presenters to convince people that they will deliver what they promise. No matter what they say or what the text slides say, words are insubstantial, disappearing from the air immediately after they're uttered or appearing lost and alone on a slide without a presenter to give them life. Prospects judge a salesperson's ability to deliver based on instinct and various visual impressions. In other words, the perception of the presenter's character will have a greater influence on a buying decision than what the text slide states.

Presenting your ideas using images communicates four things about you:

1. You're different. Using images suggests you're not like the "average salesperson." From the first visual, you're separating yourself from competing ideas, dramatically and nonverbally.

2. Your work and service will also be personalized. Tailored image presentations are more difficult to create than text slides, and they show you'll go the extra mile.

3. You're smart enough to speak without huge cue cards on the screen.

4. You're creative. Rather than presenting the same old material the same old way, you've demonstrated your ability to think conceptually. Your images reflect your imagination.

People respect individuals who exhibit these four qualities. Even without saying, "I'm dependable; I deliver," you're conveying these facts. They understand implicitly that the person who is creative, who is smart, who makes an effort, and who is different is more likely to deliver than someone who is not. Even if the images you use aren't great, your willingness to employ them gives you an edge. When you communicate visually as well as verbally, you come across stronger, with more credibility.

Seller Charisma

The French say a woman will tolerate anything in a man except one thing—that he is boring. Prospective buyers feel the same way about salespeople. Unfortunately, salespeople often commit the sin of giving a solid but mundane presentation. Few people look forward to a sales pitch. It cuts into the time to complete their work. Further, when a presenter reads 10, 20, or 50 text slides, the group wants to scream, "Stop!" Eventually, listeners tune out.

At the end of any pitch, the goal is to convince but if prospects aren't continuously paying attention, that objective is tough to achieve. Therefore, involving listeners is as critical as persuading them.

Text slides engage no one except weak presenters who are dependent on cue cards. On the other hand, with image visuals you can seize and hold viewers. As we've emphasized, images pique curiosity and cause a group to pay closer attention.

Second, you produce a feeling of anticipation—the creativity of a visual presentation causes people to think about and look forward to what comes next.

Finally, there's the "fun" factor. Images are more absorbing because they are more fun to watch than reading text slides. Another way of putting it is that images are entertaining. A clever, provocative or symbolic image can grab someone's attention in a way that no text slide can. Images convey more than just information; they stimulate another part of your mind. It's fun to look at pictures. When people are having fun, they are also in the right mood to buy or be swayed by your arguments.

When you think about images in pitches and presentations, therefore, think holistically. They can improve your selling impact on many fronts, from increasing your charisma to improving your credibility. Beyond that, they offer a host of benefits, including ratcheting up the emotional power of a presentation, making your message more memorable and grabbing people's attention. These benefits aren't just theoretical, but have been proven to exist in practice repeatedly by researchers.

Given all this, the question becomes, "why don't all salespeople use images?" We suspect the answer has a lot to do with not knowing how to create them. Fortunately, this is the subject of Part II.

PART

Getting Ready to Sell

7

Thinking Up and Evaluating Images

"Where did the idea come from that words communicate better than pictures?"

—Paul Martin Lester, Professor, Department of Communications, California State University

Most presentation software manuals treat images as embellishments. They describe how to add spinning letters, dissolving titles, or shooting stars to your presentation. They offer enticing, colored backgrounds, and design layout options—all to enhance text.

These frills and design elements have little to do with image-based presentations. In this chapter, we advise you how to express your message concisely, memorably, and pictorially. Rather than sprinkling the screen with spinning letters and shooting stars, you must focus on visualizing the message.

How to develop pictorial ideas, turn them into images, evaluate them against seven guidelines, and build reminders into your image slides are our objectives. Let's start with the process of creating images.

Creativity Is a Process and an Attitude

Some salespeople feel they lack visual creativity. As a result, they don't try to create images for use in their pitches and presentations. In reality, the vast majority of salespeople are perfectly capable of being visually creative. You don't need to be Picasso to produce slides that sell visually.

Some concepts are easier to transform into images than others. Many pictorial ideas jump to mind for the word "love." You might use a heart, cupid, outstretched arms, two people embracing, or even a suitor with his heart in his hand (Figure 7.1).

A financial concept like unfunded liability may, however, appear more difficult. If you don't tense up and worry about creating an appropriate image, you'll come up with something that works. Maybe an image of a handcuffed executive escorted into a police car? Perhaps a man's pocket turned inside out? A mortgage note? An empty purse or wallet? If you wish to stress the liability part,

Figure 7.1 Here's My Heart. . . .

consider a man or woman standing in front of a judge? Intangible concepts can be turned into viable images in many ways.

For instance, in *Creativity for Graphic Designers*, Mark Oldash (2000) identifies many techniques for generating ideas. He recommends doodling and thumbnail sketching because "the thought is captured as a pure and raw idea, not as a stylistic solution" (p. 76). He also explains that the more people look at sketches, the longer the list of ideas grows.

Let's say you're a coffee salesperson about to make a pitch to a huge, commercial foodservice operation, and you want them to buy a large quantity of your product instead of a much better-known brand. Further, you want to sell them on the richness of your coffee beans, a quality derived from growing on the slope of a mountain in the Caribbean. Therefore, you might sketch a small mountain composed of these beans. Maybe the mountain becomes a volcano with aromatic coffee bean smoke erupting. Perhaps the natives worship at the base of this coffee bean mountain. You sketch all this, and then you stare at it. Perhaps you will come up with a more down-to-earth image to use during your pitch—an actual photo of the mountainside where the beans are grown. Whatever it is, you bring out the visual idea by sketching and staring.

Collecting words is another of Oldash's recommendations: "Create a list of words and phrases that boils the problem down to the essence of what needs to be communicated" and translate them into various images. His word-generation tricks are: think in opposites, imagine colors for the words, and animate the inanimate, identify categories, and expand on metaphors. In Table 7.1, we use these techniques to generate words related to the concept *profit*. These words, in turn, suggest ways to portray that concept as an image.

You can also use existing databases and books to obtain pictorial ideas. Databases like Corbis and Microsoft's Design Live contain thousands of images that are searchable by keyword. Using concepts from the word generation exercise in Table 7.1, the Design Live database displayed images for 33 of 41 concepts.

Table 7.1 Word Generation Exercise
Using Mark Oldash's Techniques

Techniques	Words Loosely Related to the Concept "Profit," That Then Suggest Images
Metaphors	Security blanket, cold cash, warm money, money in the bank, fat wallet, Midas touch, gushing oil well, diamond as big as the Ritz, hit the lottery, money tree, piggy bank.
Color	Green as in money, "in the black," gold as a gold coin, tinfoil or lamé, platinum.
Animate	Go up, ringing cash register, multiply, speed ahead, drop to the bottom line, multiply like rabbits, double underline (as in financial statements).
Categories	Business, accounting, money, coins, economics, commerce, banking, entrepreneurship, credit, financial statements, profit charts.
Opposites	Debt, south, empty pocket, basement, dog house, flatten, loss, bankruptcy.

Develop the sequence of concepts and images before you design slides. After listing concept descriptions, you might sketch out the series of images just as advertising agency art directors prepare storyboards. This allows you to refine your pictorial ideas using the guidelines. But most important, you'll obtain initial feedback before you invest time selecting images and designing slides.

Thinking up pictorials is like doing a purely visual crossword puzzle. You might struggle for a while, try one idea, realize it doesn't fit and mentally erase it, but with a bit of effort, you'll find an idea that works.

Which Words Should Become Images?

With any presentation, you first identify the key points you want people to remember. For a 30-minute presentation, you probably have at most 5 to 7 major ideas. For an hour, you might have 8 to

12. If you identify more, you are jamming too many ideas into your pitch.

List all the ideas that support each major topic. Say you are the marketing manager for Microsoft, speaking about PowerPoint to an audience of computer store retail salespeople. For benefits, you identify:

- PowerPoint enables you to quickly format ideas into slides.
- It provides a choice of backgrounds and color options.
- It's compatible with other Microsoft office software.
- It's easy to use.
- PowerPoint shows can be displayed on a laptop, large screen, or the Web.

Here comes the critical step—deciding which ideas to turn into visuals. Dumping all of these points into bullet points is a common sales presentation reflex. Instead, choose only the top three to show as images. It's fine to mention all these points during the pitch or list them in the handout, but persuasion relies on selectivity. An unconfident salesperson pushes for quantity, a confident one for quality.

Turning Words into Pictorial Ideas

For many years in teaching design, I have taken the point of view that the creation of images is really an act of translation. You can translate English into French or you can translate English into Picture.

—Henry Wolf, advertising executive and
a former art editor of *Esquire*

Now let's refine our process for transforming words into images that sell. We've noted the first step earlier: Use techniques like word generation or doodling to come up with visual ideas. To capture them, set up a T table (Table 7.2). Under the left column entitled "Concepts," write your major points in very short sentences (include at least a subject and verb). In the right column titled "Pictorial Ideas," generate as many visual ideas as possible, both good and bad. Don't judge pictorial ideas as you jot them down. Later you'll evaluate them. For now, try to come up with three to five pictorial ideas for each major point. Next we discuss evaluating pictorial ideas.

Evaluating Pictorial Ideas

Why do some images cause only a smile while others persuade? Here are seven guidelines that help you assess the power of your pictorial ideas. Let's use the ideas in Table 7.2 to illustrate these guidelines.

1. Images Should Be Pertinent to the Topic and Audience

Sometimes you want an image to relate metaphorically to your subject. In most instances, however, you want your viewers to see a clear connection between your image and your topic. Let's evaluate the first item on the T chart—a frozen dinner, emphasizing that PowerPoint is quick (Figure 7.2). The presenter might say, "Just peel back the plastic, hit the start button on the microwave, and shortly dinner is served. By analogy, you can create slides quickly and easily using PowerPoint."

Table 7.2 Concepts and Pictorial Ideas

Concepts	Pictorial Ideas
A. PowerPoint enables one to quickly format ideas into slides.	1. Frozen dinner 2. A light bulb presenter, list, keyboard, projector, screen 3. Screen 4. Cartoon head, lightning bolt, screen 5. Keyboard, lightning bolt, screen

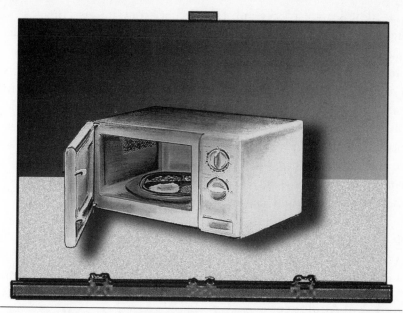

Figure 7.2 TV Dinner

While this graphic may suggest the concept of speed, it is also a labored metaphor. A frozen dinner has nothing to do with computer software. You could show the image of a speedboat, a racing car, or a cup of instant coffee, but none of these images relates to the specific product or service you're selling. Though you might use a slide like this to inject some humor into the pitch, you should not depend on it to carry your message. Always ask yourself, "How relevant and pertinent is the image idea to my viewer." If your prospects consist of restaurant managers interested in buying PowerPoint, then perhaps the frozen dinner image would work.

2. Images Should Portray the Idea Simply

Good images portray your idea simply and clearly. Like text slides, image visuals can become too busy. The simpler the image, the easier it is to understand and remember. A simple slide, however, seems deceptively easy to create. You have to work just as hard to come up with the right simple image as an enormously complex one.

The second concept on the T chart contains five images—a light bulb presenter, list, keyboard, projector, and screen. The idea is to show how quickly PowerPoint allows you to move through the steps—from raw idea to finished slide. While Figure 7.3 shows promise, the five images crowd the screen. The clutter evident in this visual should cause you to eliminate it.

Resist the urge to embellish. Unfortunately, most of us—especially aggressive salespeople—instinctively want to overdesign, to think that the more you can fit into a graphic, the better it will communicate a message. Of course, the opposite is true. As the famous architect, Mies Van der Rohe, said, "Less is more."

3. Image Ideas Must Express the Essence and Conclusion of Your Message

The third pictorial on the T chart lists only a screen. This idea, however, is vague. Yes, PowerPoint produces an image that eventually is projected to the screen. The screen image alone, though,

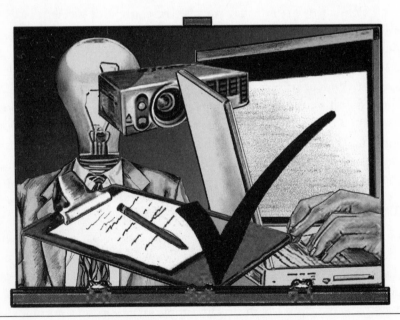

Figure 7.3 Too Much on the Slide

doesn't carry the essence of your point—how fast one can transform ideas into slides. Therefore, working through the guidelines,
we conclude that probably items four and five are the winners.
They best express the idea—slides are quickly created. Shortly
we'll discuss the differences between these two.

Now consider another example that portrays the essence but
not the conclusion. You're a lawyer talking about capital punishment. You show an image of an electric chair (Figure 7.4). It's a
simple, bold image, but lacks a conclusion—whether you were ar-
guing for or against capital punishment.

Suppose you say, "19 percent of people sentenced to death in
my state over the past 10 years have later been proven innocent
with DNA testing." You might show the same electric chair, but
add an angel pointing to the 19 percent (Figure 7.5). Now your
words and the visual carry the essence and conclusion—capital
punishment can kill the innocent.

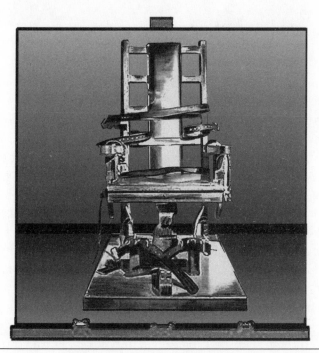

Figure 7.4 Image Too Broad

Figure 7.5 Slides Carry the Essence

Suppose you want people to draw the opposite conclusion about capital punishment. You feel murderers like Jeffrey Dahmer, Charles Manson, and John Gacy don't deserve to live. You could show the devil holding a banner with the number of these peoples' unfortunate victims. The devil depicts evil, which warrants the electric chair. Viewers leave with a firmly implanted message—in this case, atrocious acts justify the death penalty.

Both visuals reinforce your oral message and listeners carry away the strongest possible memory of it. Images aren't simply decorative. They don't just relate to your topic. They help listeners grasp the essence of your message, stir their emotions and sway them to your point of view.

Sometimes, you want an image to reveal its meaning more slowly. For example, people see the bending cigarette (Chapter 1) as you tell them that smoking causes impotency. With your words, the slide's meaning becomes clear and the conclusion obvious!

In other instances, your topic tips off the group to what an image is attempting to convey. Consider again the slide of the angel and the electric chair. Even before the presenter speaks, the electric chair suggests the message. The 19 percent figure and angelic presence likely won't be understood until the speaker makes his or her point. Because the image is recognizable but the combination puzzling, people quickly shift their attention to the presenter for the explanation. That is exactly the way most visuals should work. The image draws the attention. The presenter delivers the message.

4. Images Can Reflect Humor

Visual humor adds interest and variety to your presentation. Laughter has the power to break the ice and humanize ideas. Humor is tricky, and you should be aware that if your humor is in questionable taste, it might do more harm than good. You also need to consider what you're selling and to whom before using humor. If you're selling to a customer whom you know has a good sense of humor and appreciates appropriate gags, then you have greater license to use humor. When you use humor subtly or surprisingly, it can make your message more powerful and memorable.

5. Images Can Be Conservative or Aggressive as Situations Dictate

Images should not be randomly conservative or aggressive. You need to put some thought into the tone of your images. An aggressive approach that makes fun of a competitor may offend a prospect who has used the competitor's products for years. A conservative set of images may fail to make an impact on a prospect who is being courted by other salespeople. It's also a mistake to mix conservative and aggressive visual tones, confusing your audience about the message you're delivering.

The T chart's fourth pictorial idea lists a cartoon head, projector, and screen. Figures 7.6 and 7.7 are versions of heads.

Some prospects or customers may find that a businessperson with a flipped open head or a light-bulb face is overly frivolous;

Figure 7.6 Aggressive Heads

Figure 7.7 Conservative Approaches

that it isn't sufficiently professional. They deem these images as too extreme for their liking, and they may read into these images that you're not serious enough to serve them effectively.

If you believe your viewers are more buttoned-down than most, avoid human figures, as in the keyboard versions in Figure 7.8. This image is "safer" and unlikely to offend anyone. Of course, if you're pitching a client who is hip, daring, or open-minded, you may be better off using the light-bulb head or an even more provocative image, since they may be looking for someone who doesn't think in conventional terms. Avoid clip art and go with digital images for a serious or professional tone.

Consider conservative and aggressive approaches to another idea. Say you sell software that produces a comprehensive but lean management report. Your competitor's software provides similar information in a lengthier document. Figure 7.9 shows the conservative approach: a small stack of papers—your report, next to a larger one—your competitor's overkill.

Figure 7.8 Keyboard and Screen

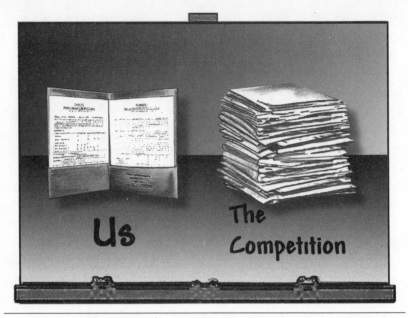

Figure 7.9 Conservative Comparisons

A more aggressive approach might show your competitor's document overwhelming the report user (Figure 7.10). Aggressive images are most appropriate for competitive or new business presentations, but you can also use them to dramatize a point in non-sales presentations or when you know your viewers are amenable to these types of images.

If you believe an approach will be more effective, go for it, but don't be mocking or cutesy about it either. It's probably best not to react to your own visual—like laughing at your own joke. Deliver your images confidently and professionally. Aggressive visuals possess entertainment value; they are usually fun and memorable. In certain situations, they can effectively differentiate your pitch from a competitor's more staid approach.

6. Use Poetic License to Make Your Point

You don't have to show images in proportion. You can exaggerate for dramatic effect. Say you're talking about pollution. You might

Figure 7.10 Aggressive Comparisons

show a mountain with out-of-proportion trash to depict the de-spoiling of our natural environment (Figure 7.11).

Maybe you're presenting the new chili-flavored pizza your test kitchen just developed. This product tested extremely well—83 percent of the focus group selected it above others. You might put enlarged chili peppers atop the pizza with the number 83 percent to the side (Figure 7.12).

Neither the trash nor the chili pepper has to be realistic or in proportion. You can visually exercise poetic license in many ways besides exaggerating the size of an object. You can do everything from giving inanimate object human traits to using surreal images to communicate a message. If you're trying to sell a corporation on using your HMO network, you might create a street map of your city and have your HMO office on every corner of every street on the map. If you're selling the problem-solving capabilities of your consulting firm, you might doctor a photo of your CEO so that he looks like Albert Einstein. In other words, you don't have to use only literal images. Most people you're presenting to have become relatively sophisticated about images—they've

Figure 7.11 Exaggerating One Element—The Trash

Figure 7.12 Chili Pizza

seen enough artfully designed ads and commercials to recognize that a visual can be used ironically, editorially, symbolically, or humorously. Therefore, don't be afraid to use your "license" to create figurative as well as literal images.

7. Crop or Come in Tight to Emphasize Your Point

Close-ups of actors' faces are often used in movies to stress a character's evil, happiness, or anxiety. To capitalize on this tool, identify the most important element you want to emphasize in a given image. Then crop the image or tighten the focus on this element.

Consider a box of cake mix. Showing the box sitting on a table has little impact (Figure 7.13). Zooming in tighter and showing much more of the box, on the other hand, makes the product the star and prevents the box of cake mix from competing with its surrounding (Figure 7.14).

With these seven guidelines in mind, let's see how images also act as cues and support your delivery.

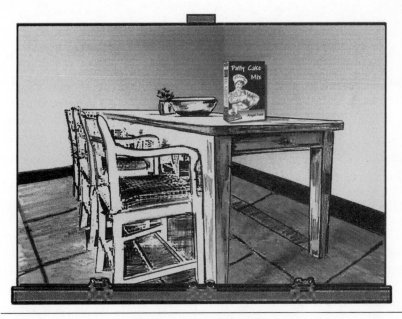

Figure 7.13 Cake Mix

Figure 7.14 Cake Mix Tighter

Integrating Subpoints into Images

Sophisticated visuals have two functions. For the viewer, images illustrate and elaborate your verbal points. For the presenter, images can remind you of what to say. Ideally, your images keep your pitch moving forward with speed and maximum impact. Here are two ways in which images can do so—incorporating mnemonics and creating visual subpoints.

Use Existing Elements as Mnemonics

A mnemonic is simply an aid to memory. You link part of the image to an idea you wish to remember. Let's return to the cake mix visual (Figure 7.15). Even a slide as simple as this one offers five visual cues: the words "cake mix," the woman on the box, the cake, the box itself, and the table. You can relate any of these visual elements to subpoints.

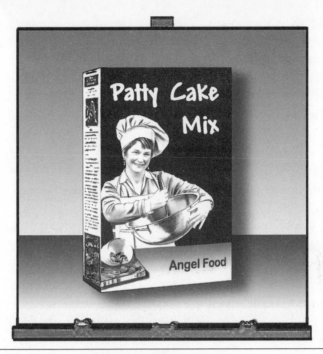

Figure 7.15 Cake Box

The woman might remind you to talk about the homemakers who buy cake mixes. Or you can mentally link the cake to why this is a sweet deal. You could associate the table with the broader market—women and men of all ages who cook.

Or you could use the letters in the words "cake mix" instead of image mnemonics. C might stand for customers and E for economics of home-baked versus store-bought cakes. The letter "M" could cue you to remember the market. With mnemonics to cue subpoints, you'll need fewer images and words per slide. This means uncluttered, cleaner visuals. For example, you won't need, in this case, another visual to remind you to cover the market because the "M" in the word cake mix can cue you for that point.

Create Visual Subpoints

Rather than use mnemonics, you can enhance images to integrate cues. Let's assume a chief financial officer is presenting budget concerns to management and wishes to include an overview or summary slide. The visual must carry lots of information but remain simple. To symbolize the principal cash drains, the CFO chooses the image of a weight lifter, struggling to hold up a barbell (Figure 7.16).

The key words express the two problem areas: sales compensation and new products. Now the presenter wants cues for the three recommendations: restructuring territories, changing commission plans, and capping the number of new items. There are numerous visual ways to accomplish this without creating a busy slide.

After choosing the straining weightlifter, the presenter creates visual reminders for the three recommendations—the ground to remember territory restructuring, the dollar sign tie for pay changes, and a hat for capping product development (Figure 7.17). It's critical that the visual not become too cluttered.

Figure 7.16 Main Points Only

Figure 7.17 Main and Supporting Cues

The image of the straining weight lifter is uncluttered and memorable, and it also contains cues for the two problems and the three recommended solutions.

Another option is a second image. It would show a smiling lifter without the weights and his hands on his hips. Now the presenter makes the recommendations off the cap, tie, and so on. This might be the benefit slide.

Minimizing Notes

We are all comfortable and fluent when we talk one to one. By minimizing notes and using screen images as reminders, you can achieve the same sincere, conversational style when you sell to a group.

Explain the weight-lifter slide to an imaginary coworker. In your own words, cover the two points (the sales compensation and product development) and then the three points (restructuring territories, changing commission plans, and capping new product development). With a few practice runs, your spontaneous delivery style, cued by images, is always more natural, friendly, and convincing than reading screen text or paraphrasing from lectern notes.

In a real presentation, you are unlikely to forget either major or minor points. You'll have bold, visual cues on the screen. As you practice with image slides, you might suddenly add a few sentences about a small point. During the actual presentation, because you are nervous, you may forget this thought. It doesn't matter. If your visual images are well conceived, your omission won't hurt the overall impact of the presentation. You are a relaxed, natural conversationalist connecting with your listeners. Images on the screen free you to speak from the heart. As we've discussed, slide reading or paraphrasing diminishes your sincerity and credibility.

Word-for-word scripts are a liability, whether on paper or a laptop screen. Most of your eye contact will be on type rather than the group. Detailed text defeats good delivery skills and diffuses your energy. Brief notes are acceptable, as you will see in Chapter 10. By relying largely on image cues, you become an extemporaneous expert. You are in control, and freed up to deliver your points persuasively and informatively.

Visuals, Variety, and Video Clips

A great presentation is a delicate balance between persuading and entertaining prospects or customers. They must be motivated to absorb content. Sometimes lawyers grab jury attention by talking as they hold up evidence—a knife, gun, or bloodstained glove.

Sellers need not have a lawyer's flair with exhibits. But they must display the same combination of information and entertainment to keep people attentive and involved. Image slides are one way presenters can do both. Selective use of video clips is another. Sellers can also employ visuals such as large mock-ups, blown-up pictures, maps, or product samples. Images come in many forms, but they all add variety and interest to presentations.

Video clips-yet another type of visual—are really mini-movies. The term refers to videos of various lengths. They may involve simple five-second animations, like the cartoon of a teacher writing on a chalkboard. They may also take the form of 30 to 40 second mini-movies, like a TV ad. They can also be longer, like movie trailers, lasting five minutes or more.

Video clips add pizzazz to you pitch. You can use them for demonstrations on how to operate a product, like the new security system. You might share with your viewers a special event, like an award ceremony. Or you could provide a visual tour of facilities or offices. If a key company executive can't attend the presentation, he or she can address the audience via a video clip.

Benefits

Who doesn't like a movie? Scenes constantly change. Action occurs. By slipping a video into your presentation, you make your pitch more entertaining. Perhaps you're covering an intangible subject, like travel. You might use a video clip with a 30-second montage of travel shots to introduce the talk.

Even if you're a good speaker, a video clip varies the pace and enriches the mix. The more variety you offer—gestures, voice modulation, image slides, and videos—the more interesting you are to people. If you're focusing on the advantages of new equipment you're selling, you can drive your point home with a concluding video clip of a live demonstration. No matter how eloquent you are about the equipment's advantages, switching to video visual mode will enhance your pitch far better than more spoken words on the subject.

Video clips make dramatic beginnings or endings. You may believe that you have to open with a visual bang to seize a "sleepy" group's attention. You may find that it's best to save your video clips for the end, especially if you have a dynamite demonstration that you want to be the last thing your prospects see. You can also pick up the pace in the middle of your presentation. If you're giving an unusually long pitch, you may want to break up the monotony of speaking with a video clip at the halfway point.

A short video can also emphasize a critical issue or product advantage. You might use a video clip to illustrate how a given product saves time or how a particular service will increase revenue. The video brings the product or service benefit to life; it's akin to underscoring a key point in black ink or drawing a circle around an important word. The video clip spotlights the benefit that might make the sale.

Though we advocate using video clips, we also advocate using them judiciously. If you overuse them, you'll dilute their impact. They can also become distractions, entertaining your viewers without selling them.

Use Clips Based on Situation and Strategy

Before you add a video clip to your talk, think about how its length will affect your message. A clip that takes a third or half of your presentation time de-emphasizes you or turns you into a projectionist. If you're trying to build credibility, you want to avoid turning your video clips into the star.

Different situations and goals influence the lengths of your clip. Let's say a new product is the highlight of your presentation. If your strategy for a pitch is to impress on prospects your track record and successes with similar clients, you may only need to show a 30-second clip of the product in order to vary the pace. On the other hand, if your goal is to give an audience an inside view of how a product actually works, a five-minute demonstration clip might be appropriate. If you feel one of your strongest selling points is the participation of a senior, highly esteemed member of your organization (who can't attend the pitch), then you might want to devote a few minutes to a clip of this individual addressing your prospects.

Whatever the length, be sure not to talk over the audio on the clip. As we've emphasized earlier, splitting people's attention is a bad idea; they don't get the full impact of the video or of you.

Requirements

To incorporate video clips, you'll need two things: a source of video clips and a well-equipped computer. Longer clips require more active computer memory or RAM, and may load slowly without it. At minimum, your computer must have a Windows 95 or higher version operating system, PowerPoint 95 or higher, a sound card, and speakers. If you wish to add sound yourself, you'll need a microphone.

To edit clips, you'll need special software. For simple editing, you can use Microsoft Media Player, bundled with PowerPoint. (It comes up when you insert an "Object" as a "Media Clip." This is not to be confused with the *Windows* Media Player, located outside PowerPoint, which has no editing functions.) More sophisticated video editing software like Adobe Premier is essential for complex editing tasks.

Are Visuals Worth the Hassle?

Are you overwhelmed by all the ideas and options involved in the creation of images? Initially, perhaps it's overwhelming, especially when you think about Murphy's Law—whatever can go wrong, probably will. Visual presentations offer Murphy so many opportunities. If you have never faced a software crash or program glitch during a pitch, you're very, very lucky. The more visuals you have, the more likely something might go wrong—an image is projected upside down or draws unintentional laughter. Why make the effort and take the risk to use images to their full potential? Fair question.

Let us respond with an equally fair question: Are your delivery skills that compelling? If you're the equal of John F. Kennedy or Orson Welles, then you don't need visual support. You can make a sale through the eloquence of your words alone.

Most of us aren't this eloquent. All these image-related enhancements, though, can increase our credibility and memorability.

When you incorporate images into your presentation skillfully, you come across with much greater impact. You don't have to be a great speaker to make a sale. You can shift at least some of the burden of selling to your visuals, and, with effort, anyone can put together a solid set of images.

So is it worth the expense, the time, and the risk to tempt Murphy? Most definitely. You gain so much selling power through the use of images that the occasional glitch and the investment of time are well worth it. And winning more often feels so good!

The Short Form

Guideline for Pictorial Ideas

1. Images should be pertinent to the topic and audience.
2. Images should portray the idea simply.
3. Image ideas must express the essence and conclusion of your message.
4. Images can reflect humor.
5. Images can be conservative or aggressive as situations dictate.
6. Use poetic license to make your point.
7. Crop or come in tight to emphasize your point.

8

Advanced Image Making

"It's better to fail in originality than succeed in imitation."

—Herman Melville

While you may feel comfortable incorporating clip art into your presentations, you may be wary of doing anything more sophisticated. You may not have resources within your organization to help you with artwork and photos. Or you are expected to put together your sales presentations on your own.

Whatever the case, we want to reassure you that you're perfectly capable of creating powerful selling imagery on your own, even if you're incapable of drawing a straight line. More than reassurance, though, we want to offer you a three-part guide for creating images that go beyond stock artwork. First we'll consider how to modify and combine existing illustrations and photos. Next, we'll look at how you can create images with your own camera rather than modify existing artwork. Third, we'll provide advice about how you can hire artists to help you with these creative tasks.

Modifying Graphic Images—
Archi Marketing

Let's assume you're the partner in a Chicago marketing firm about to make a pitch to a major real estate developer. Your firm, Archi Marketing Inc., will present its creative solutions to the developer on how to succeed in a highly competitive building market.

An assistant hands you Figure 8.1 as your title slide—the visual that will show on the screen as the eight members of the developer's committee arrive in the boardroom to see your pitch.

What's wrong with this slide? For starters, it's just the name of your company on a slide. That's boring. Besides, your firm is expected to offer creative ideas, not a visual that a 10-year-old might produce. You say to your colleagues, "What does this first impression tell the client—that we think like everybody else? That we're using our minds in an easy, predictable way? That's neither what we were engaged for nor what we produce. So why show something that neither reflects us or our work?" You redo the slide and turn it into Figure 8.2.

The ability to transform that first slide into the second, a more visually dynamic one, is not as mystifying as you may think. You'll need Photoshop or Photoshop Elements or other graphic

Figure 8.1 Archi Marketing

Figure 8.2 Archi Marketing Revised

design software to do this. Whatever you use, we'll walk you through the levels of creating this image and reveal how to use this process on your own. Here are the steps we took to create the image in Figure 8.2 that will rivet the group's attention:

1. Acquire photographs of Chicago area buildings with various shapes and heights (Figure 8.3). Go for variety to increase

Figure 8.3 Chicago Buildings

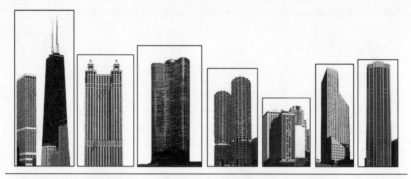

Figure 8.4 Individual Building Photos

the impact of the overall effect. Scan or download these images to the computer.

2. Strip the sky out of each of the photographs using the erase feature of the software (Figure 8.4).

3. Separate the buildings within each photograph from one another and remove any extraneous objects (Figure 8.5).

Next, we will fill in the missing sections of the building, clean up, and enhance them. Whoa! We know this is a lot of information at one time. So we'll use one building, the John Hancock, for our detailed descriptions of Steps 4 through 9. We'll change John Hancock (Figure 8.6) to look like John Hancock (Figure 8.7).

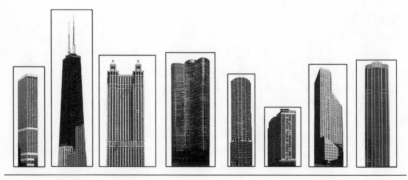

Figure 8.5 Separate Buildings and Strip Out Sky

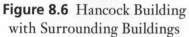

Figure 8.6 Hancock Building
with Surrounding Buildings

Figure 8.7 Hancock
Building, Cleaned Up

4. Begin with the John Hancock building in Figure 8.6.

5. Clone a section of the left side; enlarge and distort it and place it on the building's unfinished area (Figure 8.8). Save file.

6. Clone a section of the right side, enlarge and distort it and place it over the unfinished area (Figure 8.9). Save the file.

7. Clone left and right tops of building separately (Figure 8.10). Limit the angle of each by using the distortion command. Place on building and save.

8. Adjust the bottom of the building by cutting an angle of lesser degree (Figure 8.11). Trim off excess and save the file.

9. Add contrast to one side of the building to heighten the drama of the image (Figure 8.12). Copy the entire right side of the building, lighten it and place it on top of the existing building and save the file.

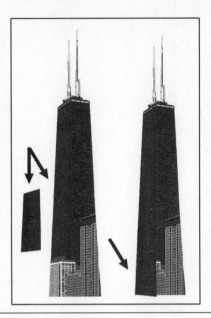

Figure 8.8 Hancock Clone Correction for One Side

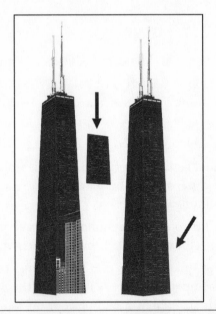

Figure 8.9 Hancock Clone Correction for Other Side

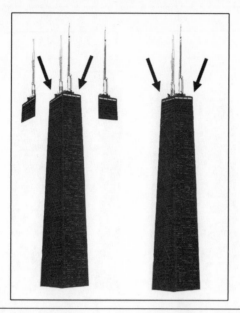

Figure 8.10 Hancock Adding Two Panels for Tops

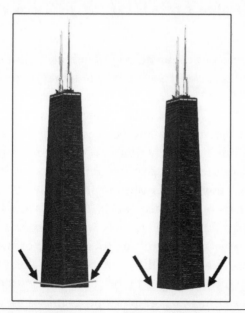

Figure 8.11 Trim Bottom of Hancock

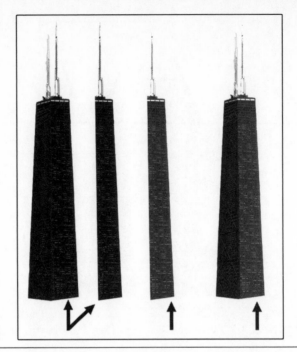

Figure 8.12 Add Contrast to Hancock

10. Use the contrast command to further intensify and the sharpen command to add crispness to the building (Figure 8.13).

By now, "Save File" should be one of your mantras. Personal experience has proven that "saving files" can prevent a load of disappointment. Oh, how many times we've labored over a wonderful image, forgot to save it because we were engrossed in the creative process and our computer crashed or froze, leaving us with the arduous task of redoing a lot of work. Also, rename the images as you do additional steps: "Hancock 1," "Hancock 2," and so on. Doing this allows you to go back to any stage of the process and make further changes for different projects. Keep in mind that saving work and cataloging it increases your resources.

Using a rudimentary graphics program, we've converted the full photo (Figure 8.14) to a partial photo (Figure 8.15) of the

Figure 8.13 Further Intensify Contrast on Hancock

Figure 8.14 Original
Photograph of the John
Hancock Building from Step 1

Figure 8.15 John Hancock
Building Following
Steps 2 through 3

John Hancock with a severe angle at its top to a completed building (Figure 8.16) and added an eye level perspective ready to be part of our composition (Figure 8.17).

Work Steps 4 through 10 on all the buildings. Each of the buildings in Figure 8.17 has been corrected, cleaned up, and sharpened. Additional contrast has been added using the contrast command. Notice that we consistently kept the left side of the buildings darker than the right. This gives the illusion that all our buildings have the same light source.

11. Now take a chess or checkerboard board from a simple graphics program. Save file (Figure 8.18).

12. Using the distortion command push in the top sides of the board and save the file (Figure 8.19).

Figure 8.16 Completed Image of the John Hancock Building Using Steps 4 through 10

Figure 8.17 Complete Steps 4 through 10 for Each Building

13. Using the distortion command again, squeeze the top and bottom of the board together to visually flatten it out (Figure 8.20). We've fashioned a compelling illusion that the chess board is getting smaller as it goes back. We've created a diminishing perspective. As usual, save the file.

14. Take an image with a hand in the correct position for playing chess (Figure 8.21).

Figure 8.18 Chess Board

Figure 8.19 Distorted Chess Board

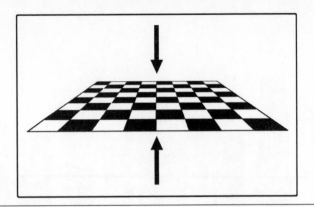

Figure 8.20 Distorted Flattened Chess Board

15. Remove the background and, in this case, the bell. Complete any missing sections of the hand by using the cloning key in your graphics program (Figure 8.22). Save file.

16. Position the hand over the chess board. Because our eyes automatically move from left to right, we reversed the hand's direction by using the rotation command and placed it in the upper right area of our layout (Figure 8.23).

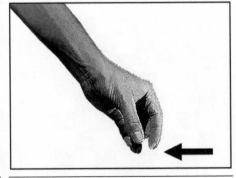

Figure 8.21 Hand for Chess

Figure 8.22 Hand without Background

Figure 8.23 Hand over Slanted Chess Board

17. Place buildings on the board and one into the hand. Add a black rectangle to the bottom of the chessboard to increase the three-dimensional effect (Figure 8.24).

18. Clone the thumb on the hand and place it over the building in the hand (Figure 8.25). This makes for a far more realistic effect. Save the file.

Nonstep: Notice that we didn't use one of our buildings in the layout (Figure 8.26). It's important to know when to stop. Don't overload your concept with needless images. Save the figure for another day . . . another project.

19. Add a background using the gradation command and a border for a more polished look (Figure 8.27).

20. Add the company logo and your opening line of copy to the background (Figure 8.28).

While our copy was the last element placed in the layout, it's by no means secondary in significance. The phrase, "Making the right move" was the inspiration for our image. We also took great care in determining the size and placement of the text or copy. Too

Figure 8.24 Hand over Buildings

Figure 8.25 Hand with Cloned Thumb

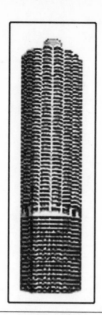

Figure 8.26 Unused Building, Marina Towers

Figure 8.27 Archi Graphic with Border and Background

Figure 8.28 Archi Graphic with Company Logo

small and it can get lost in the abyss of the buildings. Too large and it will look cramped. The empty space in the image is also worth mentioning. A good design must have enough space to breathe.

Now let's get even more creative. Here's what you can easily do with a digital camera.

Creating Photographic Images— Liberty Management

We produced the slide in Figure 8.29 for a financial management firm that manages money invested only in environmentally friendly corporations. (Name changed to protect the client.) We created this image by manipulating multiple photographs taken with a digital camera. Let's walk through this easy process.

When photographing a person, place him or her in front of a simple, mid-tone background. On your computer, you can easily

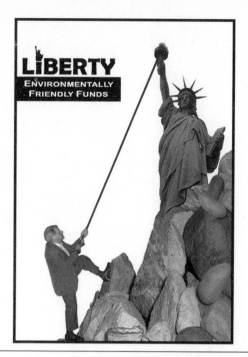

Figure 8.29 Liberty Graphic, Finished Version

remove an uncomplicated background. Using a mid-tone will keep the camera's exposure more true to the person's skin tone. If your background is white, the camera will read an abundance of light from your surroundings and you risk under-exposing your subject. If the background is extremely dark the camera could end up compensating and over-exposing your subject. Digital cameras are fabulous tools because you can review your shots immediately and make the necessary corrections. Also, keep in mind that if you want detail such as the folds in someone's clothing, have the subject wear colors that are mid-tone.

Work with the photographs in color when removing the background and other objects. It is easier to discern details in color than in black and white. While our finished samples in this book are all black and white, we worked on them in color first and than used the "grayscale" command and changed them to black and white. We did the following:

1. We photographed this man in a climbing position wearing a suit and used a scarf for his rope (Figure 8.30). In this case we did not use a mid-tone backdrop and it took a little longer to remove the background because of its complexity.
2. We removed the background and everything not pertinent in the photo and darkened his ankles for socks. We sharpened the image and added contrast (Figure 8.31).

Figure 8.30 Man, Climbing   **Figure 8.31** Man, Climbing without Background

Figure 8.32 Pile of Rocks

3. We photographed a small pile of rocks on our table (Figure 8.32). We set the digital camera to the macro setting. Most digital cameras have a macro setting for taking close upshots. It's usually designated with a flower.
4. We then removed the background (Figure 8.33). When we insert this small, five inch pile of rocks into our

Figure 8.33 Rocks without Background

image, it will take on the mammoth proportions of a mountain.

5. We reviewed our photo albums for a good picture of the Statue of Liberty from a past vacation in New York (Figure 8.34).

6. We then removed the background and base of the statue. We added final touches by sharpening the image and adding contrast (Figure 8.35).

7. We inserted the logo and tag line for our fictional financial company (Figure 8.36).

8. We enlarged the tiny rocks, making a mountain out of a molehill and placed the man climbing to its summit (Figure 8.37).

Figure 8.34 Statue of Liberty　　**Figure 8.35** Statue of Liberty without Background

Figure 8.36 Liberty Logo

9. We positioned the Statue of Liberty near the top of the peak and drew a line to suggest a rope leading to the man's hands (Figure 8.38).

10. To enhance the visual we used the sharpen command and added contrast. With all our elements in place, we positioned our company logo and copy into the layout (Figure 8.39). We remembered the design mantra throughout this entire process: "Save the files!"

Figure 8.37 Enlarged Rocks with Man Climbing

Figure 8.38 Rocks, Man, and Statue of Liberty

Figure 8.39 Composite Image with Liberty Logo

Image Resolution in PowerPoint Presentations

When working with images in PowerPoint, especially photographic images, you should understand how best to size them. According to Steve Rindsberg, if your images fill the slide, "the image size (in pixels) should be equal to the video screen's resolution. For example, if your screen resolution is set to 1024 × 768, that's the size you want your full-slide images to be. If the image occupies only half the width and half the height of the slide, it should be 1024/2 or 512 pixels wide and 768/2 or 384 pixels high.

"Highly detailed images sometimes look better if they're set at a bit higher resolution. . . . So if you're working with maps or images of text, try the same image at several resolutions" to see what works best. Remember also that the higher the resolution, the larger the image files. With large image files, your PowerPoint files will be larger and slower to display. Your images should be "just big enough to look good."

Even if you project your image on a large screen, you don't need higher resolution images. It's the resolution of the projector, not the size of the screen, that counts. Most projectors have a maximum resolution of 1024 × 768. "They may spread those pixels out over a larger screen, but the number of pixels stays the same."

In fact, "1024 × 768 is a very common resolution for laptop displays and video projectors, so it's a good choice when in doubt. The images won't be large enough to slow things down even if you show your presentation on lower resolution displays. Still, the images will look acceptable on higher resolution setups."

"This advice applies to images in PowerPoint screen shows, but it also gives you good results on most desktop printers. But for poster printouts, 35 mm slides and other high resolution output, you'll want to start with higher resolution images.

"To check your display resolution, right-click the Windows desktop, and then choose Properties. In the Display Properties dialog box, click the Setting tab. There, under Screen Resolution, you'll see the current setting. It will look something like '1024 × 768,' (meaning 1024 pixels wide and 768 pixels high)."

Working with an Artist

Your visuals do not have to be elaborate to be effective. Nor do you need to be a Van Gogh to produce an image that persuades. However, if you still have reservations about creating imagery that grabs attention, you have the option of using a freelance artist.

Local colleges have many graphic design students who can create persuasive images at a cost that is more competitive than an ad agency or a highly paid professional illustrator. Unless you are creating a proposal that is extremely demanding from a graphics standpoint, you just need someone with a moderate amount of artistic skill and experience. Another talent resource is artist coalitions and local art associations. Look for organizations in local newspapers and the phone book. You can also find numerous artists and graphic designers on the Internet. Also ask your local print shop about artists who use their services. The owner is probably familiar with their work.

At your first meeting, ask to review an artist's portfolio. Keep an open mind when reviewing their work. Whether it's a digital composition produced on the computer or a charcoal rendering executed on paper, don't expect to see exactly what you want. Most artists simply need to know what you're looking for in order to create a visual specific to your needs. Be clear with your idea and put it in writing. Be sure that artists you interview have the computer savvy to turn their work into PowerPoint slides and correspond with you via e-mail.

When reviewing portfolios you may see an illustration that is exactly what you want. Many artists are happy to resell a drawing and make additional income from it. Be creative in your thinking when evaluating their portfolio. You can create your own concept by combining elements from different pieces of their existing art work. When working with an artist on a per job basis, it is customary to make a deposit of 50 percent on the agreed-upon price for the work and pay the balance upon completion. If you hire them for an on-going project giving them a retainer is good practice. Just remember to make and sign a simple contract that the two of you agree to. It's also important to remember that you will get what you pay for. Don't expect a lot of effort out of an artist if you've badgered them to work for peanuts. Be fair!

The Selling Value of Advanced Images

Why bother? In other words, why should you worry about hiring a freelancer, manipulating photos, or juxtaposing illustrations? Do the techniques discussed in this chapter really help you make a sale?

Absolutely. You may not be convinced of this fact, even if you are convinced that visual selling makes a difference. You may recognize that these images are creative and clever, but you wonder if they really make a difference in convincing a customer to buy. You question whether an image that gets the message across with style and impact is much better than one that just delivers the message clearly.

To help you understand why these advanced images can add value, consider the three selling advantages they possess:

1. *Uniqueness:* Remember, the idea is to catch the eye, and the two approaches in this chapter do just that. You're presenting your buyers with an image that their minds have not become accustomed to. When they have seen something many times before, their minds tend to slide right over it. When they see something for the first time, though, their minds applies the brakes, stops, and takes notice. Get their attention and you have a better chance to sell.

2. *Catalyst for thought:* You want your prospects and customers to think about the ideas you're presenting. But sometimes your words don't do the trick. They may have tuned out the

sound of your voice for any number of reasons—they're tired, they're thinking about something else, and so on. However, the images we've described, that you can create through the computerized manipulations will not be ignored. They provoke people to reflect on the message you're delivering. In short, the images motivate people to take your ideas seriously and give them serious consideration.

3. *Match the message with the image:* Many graphics that salespeople use in presentations are merely adequate. They usually do a decent job of sending the right, general message, but they lack the specificity that really drives your meaning home. You're selling something different. It may be superior service, a better price, more functions, higher quality, or the best warranty in the business. You're also selling certain intangibles that differentiate you—you're more trustworthy, a better communicator, have a sense of humor. Whatever it is, an image exists that communicates your unique selling proposition perfectly. By using the advanced techniques described here, you are more likely to find the right match between your message and your image.

9

Organizing Content with Images

"Greatness is not when there is nothing more to add. It is when there is nothing more to take away."

—Antoine de Saint-Exupéry, French aviator and writer

Moving from text-dominated presentations and pitches to ones where images play a critical role is a process. As a process, it doesn't happen overnight. In fact, it's analogous to what infants go through as they transition from crawling to standing. They pull themselves up, wobble forward three steps, lose their balance, and then crash back to the floor. It's painful, necessary, and inevitable. The transition to image-focused selling may be equally traumatic for you.

Not only is it difficult to integrate the right images into a sales presentation, but it requires a highly organized approach. Some salespeople, in an attempt to use images, lose their organizational thread. They change their sequence of points in an attempt to accommodate images or the very use of graphics results in a disorganized pitch. In fact, some salespeople, frustrated by their attempt at incorporating images into presentations, fall back on a word-only pitch. This is the worst possible thing they can do.

When ancient people carved on stone tablets, their message was succinct and tightly organized because it took so much time and energy to write. With the invention of the quill and ink, words flowed easier, and writers became wordier. Then the printing press and the typewriter exponentially increased the words a person could generate.

Now with computers writers can flood readers with text. Since the advent of the personal computer, business writing has never been wordier and more disorganized. The same is true for presentations.

David Belasco, a successful Broadway producer, tells aspiring playwrights, "If you can't write your ideas on the back of my calling card, you don't have a clear idea." A calling card approach would also help create more effective sales presentations.

Unfortunately, presentation software promotes word excess. As the content expands, repetitious and irrelevant ideas mushroom and obscure the structure of too many presentations. Therefore, the key is to create a tightly organized presentation that incorporates images logically and compellingly. Let's look at how you can achieve this goal.

A Persuasive Sequence

Fixing the problem requires strong medicine. Some companies limit internal memos to a single page or constrain presentations to 30 minutes. All day venture capital seminars typically allow each entrepreneur presenter a mere 10 or 15 minutes. Restricting the length of a memo or time of a presentation, however, is the wrong approach.

The real solution is to create presentations that are tightly, sequentially organized and that limit visuals to the key idea in each sequence. The eight parts to the sequence are:

1. *Impact statement:* See Chapter 2.

2. *Overview:* Stating, up front, the essence of your message.

3. *Problem/need:* The situation and its origins.

4. *Solution/idea/strategy:* Your recommendations.

5. *Evidence:* Proof the problem exist or your solution works.

6. *Benefits:* The payoff, the reward for listeners.

7. *Easy step:* A smooth, acceptable action step.

8. *Summary:* A recap of what you've said.

Now let's explore these steps (Figure 9.1), how they fit into visual selling, and discuss their corresponding image use.

Sara Jeannette Duncan, a prolific turn-of-the-century Canadian novelist, once said, "If you have anything to tell me of importance, for God's sake, begin at the end." The beauty of an overview is it states the end, the middle, and the beginning, all in a few moments. Your listeners want to know what you're trying to sell and how you plan to sell it.

Figure 9.1 Overview   **Figure 9.2** Agenda

An oral overview not only answers this question, but it also creates a good visual start to the process. When you tell people what you're going to cover, their eyes will fix on you. If their eyes were wandering before, they'll lock right onto you as you talk about how you're going to show them that they can save 25 percent (for example) by purchasing a given service from you.

Here is an example of a good overview:

> *Let me give you a summary of what I'll cover. First I'll discuss the problem of consumers not being able to reach your customer service associates. Your call center is seriously understaffed. Almost 17 percent of the incoming calls go unanswered. You'll hear my solution that you hire two full-time employees. You really need three or four, but two would greatly reduce the complaints you're now receiving. The three benefits I'll talk about are lower employee turnover, job satisfaction and better customer coverage. And last I'll suggest that you hire two temporaries for a couple months to see if the extra coverage really starts to correct the problem. Now, I'd like to turn to the details. This presentation will take no more than 20 minutes. We'll end with questions and answers, but please feel free to ask questions as we go.*

The overview is one of those rare instances when a bullet point slide is acceptable. You don't require many bullets—a few will reinforce your message and people's eyes will quickly return to you. Instead of a deck or a handout, this simple list of bulleted points prepares people for the issues you'll address and piques their interest. It's also useful to include a few compelling images in the overview slide (Figure 9.12 on previous page). In the above overview example, you might use a caricature of an enraged customer with the phone in a death grip and his eyes bulging out of his head. Or you might show a photo of two temps in Superman capes. Whatever the image, it should revolve around the problem, solution, or benefit you're going to address.

Through your well-chosen words and images, you've hooked your audience intellectually and visually. Now you can move to the next step in the sequence (Figure 9.3), the problem.

```
┌─────────────────────────────┐
│                             │
│         OVERVIEW            │
│        PROBLEM              │
│        ────────             │
│        SOLUTION             │
│        EVIDENCE             │
│        BENEFITS             │
│        EASY STEP            │
│        SUMMARY              │
│                             │
└─────────────────────────────┘
```

Figure 9.3 Problem

Some claim there are different types of presentations—those that inform, instruct, inspire, or sell. Not true. All effective presentations should seek to persuade. Information-only presentations are a myth. Why would a speaker gather people if not to change listener behavior, open closed, lazy, or indifferent minds? What's the point of delivering information if people aren't going to use or value it?

Imagine a regional sales manager simply presenting to the newly hired vice president on why sales territories overlap. The regional sales manager who believes that this is purely an informational presentation will probably never be promoted. This salesperson has the perfect opportunity to show the vice president that he or she alone among the six regional managers possesses the enthusiasm, leadership, and creativity to be the next national sales director. In short, he is selling himself or herself.

To sell oneself effectively, he or she must present the information in a way that identifies the problem. Laying out a problem helps presenters seize people's attention. A problem almost always attracts more interest than an idea. Beachgoers don't want to hear about water safety (the idea) but a drowning (the problem) mesmerizes them.

Unfortunately, many sellers pour their energies into discussing their solution, not the problem. Of course, it's natural to do this. The solution is your brainchild. You're tempted to lavish most of your attention on your "child." Don't. The solution is an important step, but the more severe the problem, the more readily people will accept your solution.

Invest sufficient time and effort in building the problem, both through words and images. The more graphically you portray it, the more riveted people become. Use this list to think about your problem from various angles:

- How the problem developed
- How people became aware of it
- How it inconveniences customers or employees
- What the consequences are if the problem continues

Once you have identified all the aspects of the problem, you're ready to make it vivid for your viewers. Images allow you to help people grasp a problem with the most impact. You can talk about a serious problem using a conservative image or you can create a jarring, vivid image, even though you might discuss it quietly. Imagine that you are a commercial real estate broker trying to persuade the CEO of a corporation to move his offices to a new building you handle. You know that this CEO's current space is in an ultra-modern building that has won a number of design awards, but you also are aware that the design creates wild fluctuations in temperatures that aggravate everyone who works in the building. You may state this problem in words, but the odds are that this CEO will merely nod his head—you're simply stating the problem in a way it's been stated a hundred times before. Therefore, you create an image, a caricature of this CEO's employees alternately freezing and broiling—one person's hair is aflame in the image, while another is encased in a block of ice. By using imagery that hyperbolizes the problem, you ensure that the CEO understands you grasp the severity of the problem. The caricature of the building sends this message more quickly and emotionally than words can.

A vivid problem such as the one just described visually prompts the viewer to seek a solution—the one you're about to offer (Figure 9.4).

Lay out your solution in detail, using at least some of the following criteria to come up with a compelling visual and verbal response to the problem:

- A simple, concise, and complete statement of the solution
- An explanation of how it fixes the problems you've identified
- The story behind why you chose the solution you did
- Information about what it costs and what it saves
- Reference to solutions you discarded and why
- Mention of problems the solution may bring
- Outline of timetable you recommend

In addressing these criteria, be sure to search for the image that helps you deliver your solution memorably. While it may take numerous words to lay out your solution, an image flashed on the screen for a few minutes can stay in your prospect's mind for days

Figure 9.4 Solution

or weeks. A compelling image can capture the cost-saving effectiveness and efficiency of your solution in a way a million words can't.

If you're a consultant, you can talk through the night about how you will come up with more innovative ideas than your competitors. However, an image of 50 light bulbs of different colors and sizes will probably make your solution more memorable. A well-thought-out solution image can drive immediate acceptance. Done right, the problem/solution images are a potent one-two punch.

Evidence proves a problem exists or justifies your solution (Figure 9.5). Statistics, facts, similar experiences or the judgments of experts all lend weight to your evidence. However, be cautious. Evidence can easily overwhelm or appear self-serving. So you don't want to hit people over the head with it. Use images to communicate the evidence with subtlety and style. To help listeners remember your key numbers, display figures in images or incorporate them into pictograms.

The Social Security Pictogram, Figure 9.6, visually portrays the evidence: in years to come, the social security program will have fewer workers and more retirees. This is evidence that the buyer needs to purchase the retirement program you are selling. With the pictogram, that buyer can instantly grasp the significance of your numbers.

```
OVERVIEW
PROBLEM
SOLUTION
EVIDENCE
BENEFITS
EASY STEP
SUMMARY
```

Figure 9.5 Evidence

Figure 9.6 Social Security Pictogram

Present your most conclusive evidence in the image you choose and don't burden your viewers with excessive numbers or words. If you include questionable data along with convincing facts, people may discount all your evidence. Or you may spend the question-and-answer period defending an unfinished bit of research rather than furthering your idea.

Benefits are what listeners most want to hear (Figure 9.7). Evidence favors the seller—it backs or legitimizes the presenter's position. Benefits favor viewers—it's their reward for listening.

Don't confuse a feature and a benefit. A feature is an aspect of your product or solution. For example, "Every glass piece is manufactured by our company." A benefit stresses how someone is affected in a positive way. "Because we manufacture our glassware and control quality, we can guarantee you a product with superior strength and less breakage." Images help clarify this distinction.

If you think you have a benefit, ask yourself, after stating it, "So what?" Feature: We have 37 offices. So what? Benefit: We

Figure 9.7 Benefits

provide you faster service because we have a sales/service office in every major city where you have a regional warehouse.

Not only should sellers favor benefits over features, but they should tailor benefits to a given audience. For example, a seller at the National Restaurant Association packed with chefs and restaurant owners might say:

> *The unique new construction of our steel cookware jumps the temperature twice as fast inside the pan as conventional cookware, but remains cools to the touch on the outside. Your cook time is cut in half and burn accidents will drop by two thirds.*

A week later, the seller addresses venture capitalists for funding to start production. Now the speaker must change the benefits to fit the new group. For example:

> *And why is this new layered cookware important to potential investors? Because there are about 12,000 kitchen workers who receive ugly first-degree burns every year and thousands of restaurant managers trying desperately every Friday and Saturday night to push entrees faster out of the kitchen to satisfy an overflow crowd. The culinary business would welcome a simultaneous solution to the prob-*

lems of employee burns and faster cooking times. In addition let me talk about the consumer market of . . .

A month later, the presenter talks at a convention of working mothers. The product discussed is the same, but again the benefits and corresponding image are altered to fit the audience:

With the whole family eager for dinner, you'll cook and feed them twice as fast. Oh, don't forget the beautiful little arm that's always reaching up for you attention and distracts you. Never again will a pot burn you or your child.

As you tailor your benefits, remember to tailor your images. The image for the venture capitalists might include a colorful graph like the social security pictogram that projects sales to various markets. The image for the working moms might include a small child approaching a hot pan.

It's easier to use one image for all audiences, but visually, this strategy is often ineffective. We're not suggesting that you to create a different image each time you make a presentation, but most products or services have at least two or three distinct benefits, and so it behooves you to create two or three different images based on these benefits.

After a pitch, have you ever heard a decision maker say, "Good idea, but what do we do next?" This remark indicates the seller stopped selling before the finish line.

Good sellers recognize that when buyers are sold, they want to take action; they don't just want to sit there and think about what to do next (Figure 9.8). Even if you are selling in-house, you should always recommend some action step—a budget increase, an approval to hire more people, or a request for more research time. Your sales goals can be as simple as having the senior person in the room compliment your delivery skills or creative images. Always get into the habit of identifying an action step. This nudges you to think persuasively, to sell your idea or strive to enhance your reputation.

Figure 9.8 Easy Step

In life, many decisions are "yes or no," but "all or nothing" is a poor strategy in negotiating. A fear of rejection often causes sellers to end their pitches without asking for anything, hoping prospects or clients will eventually decide yes. Sometimes this works, but mostly it doesn't.

For this reason, use a technique we refer to as the *easy step*. Say your goal is to increase your department's budget for two sales support employees. Don't end with a request for the salary allocations needed, but instead set an interim goal. Ask for something less costly or controversial like enough money to hire one or two temporary employees for a month-long trial to see if the extra staff solves the problem. Or, you might ask for the time or dollars to fund an independent cost study to verify your idea.

If your request is well explained and supported, management will usually grant your request. You'll have to make a second or third presentation to reach your ultimate goal, but by helping people take this easy, interim step, you enhance your chances of achieving it. This easy step technique can work in all sorts of situations, especially when you sense that a prospect isn't ready to buy everything you're selling but needs to be coaxed along. Your instinct may tell you that he might buy a small thing, but that he won't buy the big thing without another meeting or two.

In other instances, of course, you believe you can forego the easy step and ask for the full amount or final decision. Maybe employee shortages severely impair your department's effectiveness. The problem is obvious to you and management, so you're confident management will approve your request.

Consultants use the easy step when they offer to come in and do free engineering or comment on an important in-house project. They give the client a chance to sample their knowledge. The easy step benefits both the presenter and a prospective buyer. The latter receives—at little or no risk or cost—extra time and useful information to make the bigger decision. The presenter gains partial acceptance and a second chance.

Consider incorporating an image that allows the viewer to visualize taking this easy step. Perhaps it's a photo that portrays the action you're suggesting. Perhaps you create a graphic symbol of this easy step—if you're asking a prospect to test a product on a trial basis, you show an illustration of a judge in black robes staring "judgmentally" at your product. Maybe you create visuals that illustrate three or four different interim steps that a buyer can take, using images that make their options crystal clear.

"Tell them what you're going to say. Tell them. Then tell them what you told them." Unfortunately, few follow this advice, probably because it sounds redundant. Or maybe sellers are so glad it's over and eager to sit down that they skip summarizing (Figure 9.9).

A verbal and a visual summary are critical. Repetition is good because you want listeners to retain the key points. The summary covers the same ground as the overview, but more briefly. It could be as short as four or five sentences, one for the problem, solution, and so on. For example, "In summary, as I said the problem was . . . I discussed the situation of . . . I covered the three benefits of . . . and last I asked that you . . ." Don't rush. It's your last chance for people to understand and mentally approve your message. Don't

OVERVIEW
PROBLEM
SOLUTION
EVIDENCE
BENEFITS
EASY STEP
SUMMARY

Figure 9.9 Summary

be afraid to cue your listeners that you're about to end your pitch. Start your summary with phrases like "In summary" or "In conclusion." This draws people's attention not only to your words but your physical presence.

Take advantage of this visual attention by using an image to reinforce your verbal summary. Your participants remember best what they last hear and see. This is your final chance to imbed in your listeners' minds your insights, and recommendations. If you can't think of a unique summary image, simply use a second copy of your solution or benefit image. Label it "Summary." Leave this slide up during your entire oral wrap up and during the question and answer. It's the last slide your prospects see so it's the most likely one they'll recall.

Using the Time Wisely

Sellers often end up with too much material for the presentation time slot. Unfortunately, few presenters have the fortitude to simplify and edit. They fall in love with their material and can't bear to ditch supposedly brilliant points or beautifully prepared slides. Just as trimming personal or corporate expenses takes guts, so does eliminating presentation content.

It's important to state in your opening remarks exactly how long you'll talk. Obviously this puts a burden on you, as it should. It's your responsibility to stay within that time limit.

A seller's credibility plummets in direct proportion to the length he or she spills over the limit. Prominent politicians or egotistical executives often feel free to exceed such limits. They may also feel they can bombard their viewers with a slew of text slides, disrespecting people's tolerance for sensory input. In either case, these pitches come across as either poorly organized or inconsiderate.

Let's say the boss, prospect, or client gives you 30 minutes for your pitch. If, after you practice several times, you're convinced you only have 20 minutes of content, don't worry and don't try to pad 10 minutes. In your overview, simply state you will talk for about 20 minutes and leave the remainder for the group's feedback. People love short presentations and appreciate that you've planned time for their questions, comments, or feedback.

If, on the other hand, you find you have a full 30 minutes of material, don't celebrate too early. Presenters, especially inexperienced ones, often talk faster during an actual presentation because they are nervous. A nervous speaker will finish 30 minutes of material in 20 or 25 minutes. Don't be thrown by this; simply move into questions.

If you're an excellent presenter, the opposite may occur. You'll get comfortable and folksy. The 30 minutes can easily become 40 or 45. Avoid this. Listeners rarely appreciate going longer. Cut your 30 minutes of material to 20. By weeding and tightening, you'll emphasize your key points and stay within the time limit even if you get folksy.

When you organize with images, they carry a sizable part of your message. Your words are certainly important, but "fewer" are better than "more." So don't extend your welcome!

The Eight Persuasive Steps

1. *Impact statement:* See Chapter 2.
2. *Overview:* Stating, up front, the essence of your message.
3. *Problem/need:* The situation and its origins.
4. *Solution/idea/strategy:* Your recommendations.
5. *Evidence:* Proof the problem exists or your solution works.
6. *Benefits:* The payoff, the reward for listeners.
7. *Easy step:* A smooth, acceptable action step.
8. *Summary:* A recap of what you've said.

Selling Situations

CHAPTER

10

Selling to Different Groups and in Different Situations

"In order to be irreplaceable one must always be different."
—Coco Chanel, French fashion designer

U p to this point, we have focused on general visual selling principles and techniques. Now, we will focus on how to apply these techniques in different settings. The visual approach in a competitive presentation differs somewhat from seminar selling. The visual setups that work in a trade show forum need to be adjusted when you are selling to a large audience. Selling your ideas to enhance your professional standing requires an entirely different visual concept.

Maybe you are selling to one particular group at this point in your career. However, we can almost guarantee you that you are going to have opportunities to sell to many types of groups. All it takes is one job promotion. Now, instead of selling one on one exclusively, you are suddenly selling to larger groups. You may be invited to speak at a trade show or you may find yourself running a workshop and attempting to persuade the attendees to adopt certain beliefs or establish a network of referral sources.

Whatever your situation, you must always know the best visual approach. The material in this chapter helps you learn it.

Competitive Presentations

Competitive presentations are a beauty contest, a chess game, and the Olympics of selling, all rolled into a single pitch. In fact, there are so many things to think about, some salespeople forget that they can persuade visually as well as verbally. Let's examine the critical factors that will help you win a competitive pitch, with an emphasis on the visual.

The Good Old Boy Approach

This is our name for a casual selling approach. It's laid-back, folksy, and appeals to salespeople who believe it will help them compete against a formidable tie-and-pinstriped team. They may think a "let's just sit around the table and talk" style is strategically sound or they may be lazy, but whatever the motivation, this approach rarely works.

Why? Because competitive presentations start as a beauty contest. Clients want to see you at your best because your best is what they expect you to deliver if you win. They have not invited you in to hear unprepared, unrehearsed, off-the-cuff advice.

More to the point, a beauty contest by definition is a visual experience. You need to put your best face forward. In highly competitive pitches, the difference between what you have to say and what another salesperson communicates may be negligible. You may be offering a roughly comparable service or product at a roughly comparable price. What differentiates you is often the impression you leave, the sense of your commitment, energy and creativity. That impression often is formed visually.

If you're sitting to sell in a good-old-boy informal style, then you will have trouble making a visual impression. Standing is always better than sitting. When you stand, you have more of a canvas to work with. Not only are you in a more dominant position than a seated individual, but your whole body shows. You can gesture with greater authority; you can communicate with your posture; you can use your "taller" stance to draw the spotlight to you.

At the same time, a formal pitch allows you to incorporate images into the mix. As we've emphasized, they offer variety, retention, and most important, they reflect that you have gone to a lot of trouble to tailor the pitch to a particular customer. In addition, you will need customized handouts to remind clients how special you believe they are. All this effort shows you at your best. It communicates that you care enough to do your homework and that the good old boys sitting around a table don't.

If you're selling one on one, of course, it would be awkward for you to stand while your prospect is sitting. Nonetheless, just because only two of you are in the room doesn't mean that you should wear overly casual clothing, slouch in your chair, or fail to incorporate images into your presentation. If you allow selling to devolve into a casual conversation devoid of visual elements, you probably won't be pleased with the outcome of this conversation.

Crafting a Visually Competitive Message

Let's say you're competing against two other companies. You know one of them is going to emphasize how they are the biggest supplier and the other is going to tell them that they offer the lowest price. You can't make either claim, so what can you say?

In many instances, you're going to be speechless, at least in the figurative sense. You can and should talk about the quality of your customer service, your commitment to meeting customers' needs, and your track record in these situations. What really will drive home these points memorably and impactfully, though, are the images you project in your pitch. Here's how to build a visually competitive message.

First, determine the one word that differentiates you from your competitors in a positive way. Limit the differentiator to one word. Perhaps it's "solid." Maybe it's "trustworthy." Whatever that word is, that is your clue to how to present visually. You want every visual element of your pitch, from the clothes you wear to your gestures to your graphics, to convey this word.

Then, explore different ways of expressing the word using all the visual tools at your command. Let's say you choose trustworthy as your key word. What type of attire will communicate that you can be trusted? Not a leisure suit, certainly. Not anything flashy or cheap. Instead, you and all members of your team must agree on attire that subtly but surely suggests that you are honest and straightforward.

Similarly, you should create a list of graphic possibilities that cohere to project trustworthiness. It might be a single image repeated in different ways or a series of images that build toward the conclusion that you're to be trusted.

Check to see that your visual theme, in fact, carries through. Gather a few colleagues in a room and do a dress rehearsal of your pitch. Then, after you're finished, ask them to answer the following questions:

- How would you characterize our gestures during the pitch; did they seem to invite trust and respect; did they seem overly aggressive; were they wimpy?

- Do you remember a single visual from our pitch; what is the first word that comes to mind when you think of the images you were shown?

- Think back to how we "appeared" during the pitch. Forget what we said for a moment and just think of our clothes and our expressions. Pretend you didn't know what we did for a living and were asked to say what profession we represented visually. Would you say we most closely resembled: (1) Used car salesmen, (2) Bankers, (3) Manufacturers, (4) Lawyers, or (5) Entrepreneurs?

Delivering a "Wow" Factor

Remember, it's a beauty contest, so do something visually special—very special. For example, instead of just the normal two presenters, consider bringing a larger or more impressive team to the presentation. Ask your CEO or the head of customer service to accompany you. Maybe include an important client in your pitch who believes you provide exceptional service—have a videotaped testimonial or bring the client to the pitch. Or include a prop that demonstrates how your prospect's product benefits from your advice or service. Think about doing something out of the ordinary that tells the prospect you view this opportunity as significant. A "wow" visual approach does that.

Remembering the Easy Ones

Competing is tough. Don't miss the simple visual lay ups. The easy shots are the room set-up elements—the screen angled to the side, leaving the lights on, sitting prospects in the right chairs, standing with the screen to your left, and others. Make sure one team member handles renting the portable screen, checking out the room light switches, electrical outlets, and every other detail.

Practicing the Right and Wrong Rehearsals

When your team members gather, do they practice an oral or visual rehearsal or both? A common rehearsal mistake is to run through only the words. As team members gather to rehearse their content, you should insist that each presenter also practice gestures, eye contact, pauses, and enthusiasm. No exceptions, even for the senior partners!

Remember, too, that the visual rehearsal should not be an afterthought. Don't wait for the last rehearsal to practice these elements, since people won't invest enough time and practice to break bad visual habits.

Listening Instead of Talking in Question and Answer Sessions

Earlier, we addressed best visual practices in question and answer (Q&A) sessions, but we want to emphasize one critical issue that arises in highly competitive presentations:. Here especially, it's wise for the prospect to talk and ask questions while you listen and respond only briefly. Unfortunately, when competitive teams step into the "ring," they often overwhelm the prospect. They do so not just verbally but also visually. Here's how it happens.

The prospect asks a question. The appropriate team member answers it, but the team leader wants to reinforce the answer. Then a third team member adds his or her opinion. Now we have three sellers who are talking, gesturing, and standing for a significant percentage of the Q&A period, which conveys that you're not paying enough attention to the prospect.

Try hard to follow the rule—one question, one answer. As a seller, you gain far more from hearing the questions than answering them. Therefore, make sure you don't visually dominate the Q&A session by limiting the number of responders so clients can ask more questions.

Seminar Selling

"How to maximize retirement income," "The value of long-term care insurance," and "Avoiding probate with a living trust"—are just a few examples of seminars that provide opportunities to gain new business—if presented visually. But, they rarely are. Invariably those who conduct these seminars forget a key point: they walk a fine line between entertaining and connecting with listeners—not unloading an information dump. To entertain and connect, sellers must integrate visual elements into their presentation, using the power of imagery to keep their audience's attention as well as to make a memorable impression.

Entertainment

People don't give up their free time lightly. If they make the effort to attend your seminar, you better be sure their attention doesn't wander during the lengthy period of time in which you conduct it. Images can create a sense of excitement, can add humor and can draw people into your points. Text slide after text slide, on the other hand, will fail to achieve any of these goals, no matter how valuable the information conveyed might be. Image visuals get you half way through a successful public seminar because they entertain and keep the focus up front.

Speaker Expertise

The goal of a public seminar is often to get participants to connect quickly with a speaker they probably don't know. This means more than establishing a brief moment of connection when your audience laughs at a joke you tell or responds with applause to a point with which they agree. The key is continuous connection, and having a visual strategy is essential if you want to make this connection. Only a commanding presence can do that.

Do not hide behind a lectern. In building trust, no mental or physical barriers must exist between you and your audience. Viewers buy into you and your advice because they see that you are trustworthy, inspiring and sincere. An expert must appear comfortable and natural. You are the most important visual element in the room and must act accordingly. You will need superior delivery skills—especially gestures and enthusiasm. They'll help you draw attention, connect and sell your ideas to viewers.

Two critical visual elements drive successful public seminars— entertaining images and the presenter's dynamic delivery skills. Concentrate on these two and you'll definitely increase sales from public seminars.

Trade Show Booth Selling

The best way to sell visually behind a convention booth is to understand the problem your prospects face. Pretend for a moment that you are a typical attendee seeing hundreds of booths. As you cruise the aisles, you glanced left and right, attempting to decide which booths warrant closer attention. This is tough to do. You usually have lots of ground to cover. At a hurried pace, you walk and scan both sides of an aisle. As you sweep your eyes back and forth, you probably look at each booth for less than a second.

As you put yourself in the place of the trade show attendee, recall that images are comprehended much more quickly than words. Your eye takes in a beach instantly but comprehending the same scene described in words would require much more of your time. Similarly, visual distinctiveness catches the eye far more surely and quickly than text plastered on booth walls. Despite these truisms, the typical convention booth projects its message almost entirely in words. In the one or two seconds that your eyes scans the text of each booth, you cannot possible take in its message.

A booth has only one purpose—to draw attendees into the space so salespeople can greet them and begin selling. At car shows, many of the car manufacturers have figured out that displaying the latest vehicle on a rotating platform under brilliant lighting will attract a crowd. They have also recognized that adding another visual element—an attractive woman—will provide an almost irresistible one-two visual punch, at least to certain types of male attendees.

Image Examples for Booth Design

If you wish to draw qualified, potential buyers to your booth, design your space so that images drive 80 to 90 percent of your message. For example, you make widgets and your latest model can withstand 10 times more pressure and heat than last year's version.

Consider the following image. A large illustration or photo of a heavy military tank with its moving treads made with your widgets. A software program like Photoshop can easily add your widgets into a photo of tank treads. The words above the image might say, "Our New, Indestructible Widgets." Remember, it's 99 percent the image that stops the attendee in front of your booth. The title is only 1 percent of the attention-getting factor.

Here's another image that might work well for this widget booth: a fearsome, multicolored, fire-breathing dragon. In front of the beast sits an anvil with a dozen of your oversize widgets unevenly stacked. The dragon has just blasted the anvil as smoke and bits of fire still hanging the air. The anvil appears slightly deformed from the intense heat barrage. Your widgets, of course, sit as shiny, indestructible pieces. The words displayed across the top read, "Our New, Heat-Resistant Widgets."

Image Guidelines for Booths

Create the simplest possible image for your booth, just as you would with a slide. In the half second that attendees scan your images, don't let them struggle with the visual interpretation. For example, you don't want them to think, "Um, nice penguin and icemaker, but let's see . . . the marshmallows on the stick by the fire must mean . . ."

Before you imprint any booth visuals, show a sketch of your image ideas to colleagues and friends. Don't worry if they don't know what your company's does—many of the people who pass by your booth will be similarly in the dark. Leave the title words off the paper. Ask your "test subjects" to give you their instant associations and interpretations. If they have to study it for more than a few seconds and ask questions, the image is most likely too complex and not suitable for a trade show booth (or a presentation).

As you think of images for your booth, write a list of important benefits. Then decide on only one benefit that you want to feature. In the widget example, you would not want to communicate that your widgets are indestructible, heat resistant, and color fast. That would make your image too complex. Instead, pick the benefit that will have the broadest or strongest appeal or spark the most interest to convention attendees shopping for your type of produce or service. However, you certainly could use brightly colored widgets in either the tank or the dragon image, covering two benefits. But the emphasis should be on one—indestructibility or heat resistance.

Images, not booth walls of text, stop attendees and pull them into your booth.

The Traveling Seller

The stress and strain of traveling often discourages schlepping computers and projectors. A few equipment breakdowns may discourage you from bringing the components necessary for electronic visual selling. If you prefer to go the low-tech route, you can still put together an effective visual pitch using art boards or flip-chart sheets.

To create visuals for boards or sheets, produce images with your presentation software. Back up the image slide files to a disc and print a paper copy for your reference. Now e-mail or take the disk to companies like Kinko's and Alpha Graphics. Or look up a company in the Yellow Pages under laminating, blueprints, or color photo enlargements. The firm you choose must be able to blow up your images on to foam boards, poster boards, or loose sheets. Let's consider the advantages and disadvantages of boards or loose sheets.

Formats

Lightweight, rigid, foam boards stand up nicely on an easel stand. Poster boards are thinner, but are floppy and bow on an easel stand. The deciding factor between the two is how many boards you need. You can comfortably carry about 10 to 15 of the thicker foam boards. With thinner poster boards, you can fit more in a carrying case, but the load quickly becomes heavy.

To decide between the two, go to an artist supply store and look at portfolio carrying cases (Figure 10.1). Fill the largest

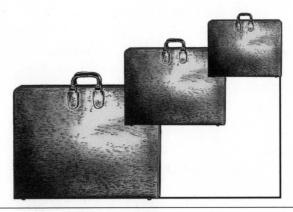

Figure 10.1 Portfolio Carrying Case

case with foam boards, then with poster boards. These big, blank boards probably won't allow you to zip the case, but you can feel how much they weigh and how bulky they are. (The production house will supply the boards, reproduces your artwork, and size the boards to fit the case you buy at the artist supply store.)

Because thinner poster boards buckle when placed on an easel stand, they'll need support. You can do this with a single foam board. Leave it as a backstop and as you pick up each poster board, clip it to the foam board. It's annoying to clip and unclip each visual, but you must take this step if you show a dozen or so poster boards. Resist talking as you clip and unclip to avoid dividing your message.

Loose, oversize paper sheets are light and very portable. Usually you can order these larger, easel-size sheets from a printer who buys them from a specialty paper wholesale house. Sheets, however, will become "shop worn" faster than boards. Artist supply stores sell a tube case with a shoulder strap to carry loose sheets. During your presentation, you may hang sheets or clip them to a foam board.

The Da-Lite Oravisual company manufactures a good easel stand, with a T-bar clamp, for both loose sheets and poster boards (Figure 10.2; Model #D305 or #43165; Phone: 800-622-3737 or see Da-lite. com to locate a retail dealer).

Size

Bigger is better with art boards, but remember your carrying case limits the board size. Cases don't come much larger than 30 by 40. Therefore, your boards shouldn't exceed this size. For a group of up to 20 viewers, the boards can be smaller—23 by 23 works. Alternatively, many loose sheets easily fit into a tube carrying case.

For larger groups, it helps for you and the boards to be on a stage or at least a riser. This portable metal platform elevates you a couple feet off the floor. Again, you're at the center with the easel stand, which is angled and at your left, positioned like a portable screen.

Figure 10.2 Stand with T Bar Clamp

When you speak to around 60 people or more, boards become too small for back row viewers to see effectively. For big audiences consider fighting Murphy again and moving to PowerPoint slides on a screen.

Selling to a Large Group

You may have the opportunity to sell to hundreds or speak to 50 people at an in-house program. As a speaker, your goal may be indirectly to pitch your produce or service. Or maybe for an in-house setting, your objective is to "sell" employees on a new software system that they have been reluctant to use.

For instance, let's assume you're a sales representative for a high-tech security firm and one of your products is identity recognition software based on body characteristics. You are invited to speak to 600 people who are attending a security conference. Your audience consists of corporate, government, and science lab security directors who are your target market. One of their big concerns is verifying the identity of those entering a research lab or sensitive production area. Biometric technology has been changing rapidly, using fingers, palm, face, and eyeball recognition. Since your company has led the trade headlines with retina and iris scans, you will address that type of biometrics.

You can't outright promote your company's system. However, you can speak about the merits and advantages of eyeball identity. This presentation, done well, should net you lots and lots of business cards—people who request that you follow up with them. Let's examine the two ways you can take advantage of this opportunity—the conventional verbal sales approach or the uncommon visual one.

The Deadly Verbal Approach

Writing out your presentation is a challenge in and of itself. Delivering that speech effectively, however, dramatically ups the ante. You'll need to memorize large parts of the document so you can give plenty of eye contact to the audience. Memorizing the entire talk, especially if it's relatively long, is very difficult for most people. The alternative—reading the script—will quickly lull the audience to sleep. Assuming you don't have a photographic memory or aren't a polished script-reader, here are three skills you need to master:

1. *Eye contact:* The moment most presenters mispronounce a few words and feel the adrenaline surging through them, they panic, hunker down, glue their eyes to the page, and concentrate only on correctly reading the words. Or they may look up every so often, but their rapid glances betray their nervousness. Not maintaining eye contact quickly disconnects the speaker from the audience.

2. *Gestures:* Most lectern presenters grip the sides of the box and tightly hold on. It's just them, their nervousness, and the

script. It's a standard pose. With no action (gestures) at the lectern, people in the audience slightly bend down their heads, tune out, and think about personal or business matters. They won't miss anything visual and can still hear the voice from the box.

3. *Voice:* It takes a pro to read and continuously vary his or her voice level. Most lectern presenters concentrate so hard on just stringing the words together and not mispronouncing any that they soon drop into a monotone. A flat voice always causes a gestureless body and disconnected eyes. Listener boredom quickly follows.

We hope we've painted an ugly picture. The odds are heavily stacked against standing behind a lecture and successfully delivering a script. With a verbal approach, the mind concentrates on the written words, while seriously neglecting voice variation, eye contact, and gestures. Tying yourself to a script almost guarantees you will not connect to the audience. Let's get out of this minefield and into the visual approach, which you can control much easier.

The Persuasive Visual Approach

The visual approach works for one simple, but often overlooked fact. All of us speak extemporaneously one to one. From experience, we can claim success in hundreds, thousands of daily conversations. (Most of us have very little, if any, experience speaking from written scripts.) Capitalize on your experience in these situations and translate it to a visual, large group approach.

Briefly, here is the visual approach. Begin by stepping away from the lectern and delivering your presentation. You are completely supported by cue cards—not in your hands—but lying on the lectern. Very shortly, we'll explain how this works. But first a few words on how the style of one-to-one conversations applies directly to large audience presentations.

You often talk without notes for 30 or 40 minutes when conversing with friends, colleagues, or even strangers. For example, you're on a long plane flight. You introduce yourself to the person next to you who says, "What do you do for living?" You quickly summarize your specialty, identity recognition. He says, "Interesting. Can a machine really recognize an eyeball?" How long can you carry on that conversation? An hour? Four hours? You'd have no problem enlightening your seatmate, right? The conversation would just flow. You wouldn't even think about it.

Achieving the same smooth flow when you're nervously standing in front of 600 people presents a challenge,; but it's very doable. The technique involves extending your extemporaneous conversation to a large audience with the backup of cue cards.

The whole idea is to position you as the dominant visual in the room. It's about you and your ability to deliver a persuasive message with emotion and conviction. You perform very well one to one. Here's how you can do the same in front of 600 faces.

A cueing system keeps you on track even if your memory momentarily blanks out. Say your "identity" talk is to run 45 minutes. You will have between 8 to 12 major points. (If you have more than that, you're probably packing in too many ideas.) On 5 × 8 cards turned vertically, write each major point at the top of the card. Use only one to three words to prompt each thought.

Create a word or two that cues a key topic for about every five minutes of content. Next, talk your way through that five minutes. Then break the five minutes into two or three sub points. You now have a reminder word or phrase for every few minutes. For example, your first 5 × 8 cue card looks like Figure 10.3.

You would start with a few introductory remarks that you should memorize. This lets you establish good solid eye contact right up front. Then you pause, look down, and the card cues you to cover how each human iris is "so unique that no two irises are alike even among identical twins, in the entire human population, and so on." You continue to cover the rest of the retinal ID information. Of course, one to one, you would reel off all this without even thinking.

Figure 10.4 is your second card. You're going to talk about Dr. Daugman's work and how "the iris has six times more distinct identifiable features than a fingerprint."

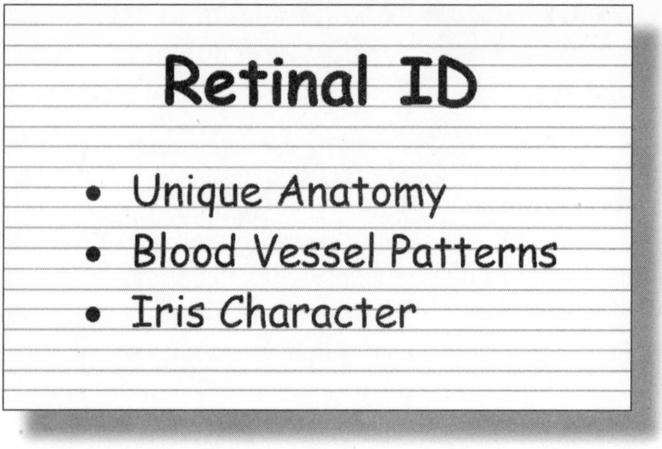

Retinal ID

- Unique Anatomy
- Blood Vessel Patterns
- Iris Character

Figure 10.3 First Card

This card carries information that would be easy to forget or recall. For this reason, it's a good idea to place important numbers, statistics, or names on your cue cards. Include in this "forgetful" category any subtopic that you keep stumbling on during your rehearsal or can't quite remember to say each time you rehearse with that card.

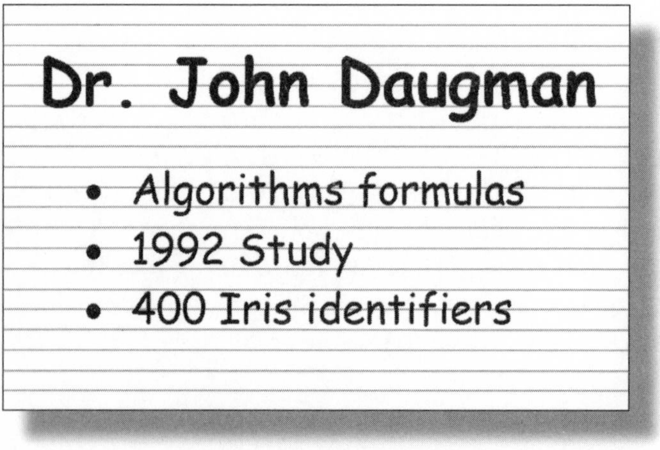

Dr. John Daugman

- Algorithms formulas
- 1992 Study
- 400 Iris identifiers

Figure 10.4 Second Card

Cue Card Guidelines

Here are some do's and don'ts for your cue cards:

- *No script:* Please don't write any sentences on these cards. Just a few words. The idea is that if you need reminding, you'll pause, look down and instantly "get it" without having to "read it."
- *Big:* Fill up each card. No small type or print.
- *Number:* Number the cards in the upper right hand corner. If they fall to the floor in the cab ride or on your short walk to the lectern, you can quickly return them to the right order.
- *Slide reminder:* Place a reminder above each topic where a slide should project. For example, a notation like V-1 in Figure 10.5 cues you to change slides. Circle it with a red marker or point an arrow to it.
- *Gripper:* Bend up a 1-inch section of the 5 × 8 card's lower right-hand corner. This allows you to easily pick up and turn it over when you're finished with it.

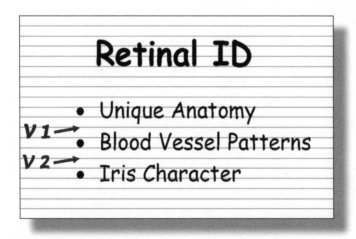

Figure 10.5 Slide Changing Cues

Rehearsing for the Big Pitch

This type of presentation is so important that we strongly recommend at least a dozen rehearsals. You might get the words down after a few practices, but it takes more than a few to get all the visual elements (gestures, pauses, etc., and the changing of your images) in synch. By the tenth rehearsal, you should only glance down at each cue card two or three times. That's acceptable retention and will provide you with the comfort zone you need to concentrate on your delivery skills.

Don't create visuals until you run through three or four rehearsals. Master the content before you commit to any images. By the third or fourth rehearsal, start firming up ideas for visuals. If your slides aren't yet ready, on the fifth and sixth rehearsals, practice with imaginary visuals. Stand at a blank wall and use gestures to lead viewers through the imaginary images. Then pause and physically go through the motions of changing the slide. Do this slowly just as if it were the actual presentation.

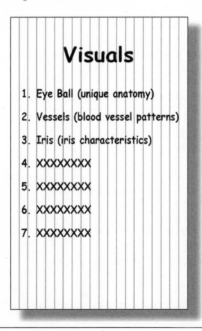

Figure 10.6 Card Showing Slide Order

After you complete your slides, take a 5 × 8 card or two and list your visuals (Figure 10.6).

This list, next to your cue cards, helps you see your slide order. Also, it can help you during Q&A to quickly reference and retrieve a slide that a questioner refers to.

You can insert this list and even your cue cards as notes to yourself in PowerPoint. However, if the electrical power goes down or your computer dies, you're cooked. With your slides on a disk, a hard copy of your visual list, and your cue cards, you have a better chance to recover and keep going if disaster strikes. If your computer crashes, you can still give a presentation with just your 5 × 8 cue cards or a standby computer you have rented.

Your last few rehearsals should include finished slides. Wear your presentation clothes. Do the shoes pinch? Does your suit coat move with your gestures? Have colleagues and friends watch and critique you. The point of rehearsals is to leave nothing to chance, especially the visual elements that are under your complete control. Your goal is not to simply get through it, but belt a home run—far out of the park.

Come Out of Hiding

Consciously or not, some people use the lectern as a shield between themselves and the intimidating large number of people to whom they're speaking. If you're going to be a strong visual seller, you must step away from the lectern. The lectern was made for only one thing: to hold the speaker's notes. It was never meant to hide behind but ironically, most speakers love a lectern. Their shaking legs don't show. They can steady their trembling hands by tightly gripping the sides and concentrate on reading. This produces the worst possible presentation. Use the lectern only to hold your cue cards, visual list, and laptop or slide changer.

In rehearsals, start your presentation half a step away from the lectern. The screen is half a step to your left. Position yourself in the open space between the screen and the lectern. The first words you say are the impact statement. Now you continue until you blank out or need to change a slide. In either case, you pause for a full two seconds, as you slowly but deliberately move half a step right, back behind the lectern and cue yourself or project a slide.

Don't rush either of these moves. The audience members are already impressed that you are speaking without notes. They fully expect you to occasionally step back and check your direction or refresh your thoughts. If you rush, you're liable to look down too quickly and start charging ahead with major point C rather than B. Look down, verify the point you need, and continue to pause as you move back to your speaking position. Don't walk and talk. This will force you to take the full pause and execute correctly.

Remember not to speak as you do anything physical—change a slide or chart board or turn the flip chart. We know it's hard to forget the role of college professors with their backs to us writing on the blackboard as they lecture away. But, doing two things at once divides your concentration. Your voice will drop and you'll loose eye contact. You are not giving your full attention to the viewers, the physical act, or your content. Remain completely silent when you undertake anything physical.

In your "working with the slides" position, stand a full step away from the lectern. That puts your left shoulder almost touching the screen. Your left arm works with the image that you're explaining to the audience. You summarize the slide and transition to the next image. Then you pause and move the full step back to the lectern. Continue pausing as you verify that you're hitting the right key. Hurrying to change the slide and frantically pushing the wrong keys has resulted in some humorous errors like mistakenly bringing up little Martha's birthday pictures.

When you deliver away from the lectern, three key benefits occur. First, you connect very personally with the group. Second, you present the experienced, real you, conversing one to one. And third, this "no hiding" position allows you to channel nervousness into positive visual energy—gestures and enthusiasm.

Checking Out the Site

If ever an occasion existed that warrants showing up a full day ahead, this is it. Here are some visual-related points to include in your checklist:

- *Rentals:* Before you leave home, search the Internet for companies in the location where you'll speak that rent screens, backup laptops (if yours fails), wireless clip on mikes, and projectors, as well as temporary personnel agencies. If you're not absolutely comfortable with what is furnished on site, immediately go rent what you need.

- *Being seen:* Will the hotel ballroom or the convention center auditorium provide a riser platform? A riser elevates you a few feet above the audience so you are well seen.

- *Screen:* Is the screen furnished? If so, is it too big or too small? If the furnished screen doesn't exactly fit the audience size, rent one.

- *Cables:* Are computer connector cables compatible and available? If not, you're in big trouble! Don't wait until show time to find out.

- *Spare bulb:* Are you carrying an extra projector bulb? Bulbs don't burn out sitting in the closet.

- *Furniture instructions:* Give the convention coordinator a layout of how you want the screen and lectern positioned. Remember, you're in the center, the lectern to your right and the screen to your left and angled. (Invariably it will be set up wrong. Remember Murphy?) It's your opportunity, your reputation. You have every right to rent (probably at your own expense) or request what it takes to make your talk unfold successfully. Both you and the association want that.

- *Temporary help:* Consider hiring a temporary person to help you do one very important function—distribute your handout after the presentation. Mention in your introduction that your assistant will pass out, at the end, a complete handout (hold it up and show it). Keep the boxes of handouts up front by you, so no one will walk out with one five minutes after you start speaking. The handout is a small reward for hearing your whole talk. Also say that the assistant will collect business cards with questions or comments on the back for those that must leave before you finish or immediately afterwards.

At the end of the presentation, have the assistant come up front to pass out the handouts. Have him or her stand at the opposite side of the stage from you. This brings people to the area you are standing but away from where good, qualified prospects are waiting to talk to you.

We've shown you how to display the greatest visual asset you have—yourself. Now let's end by discussing the best presentation partners you could choose—images.

Simplifying Images for a Large Audience

Here's the scenario: You are the senior marketing executive in charge of military sales for a computer software company. You're a decorated 1990 to 1991 Gulf War veteran, a graduate of one of the military colleges, and active in the reserves. Early in your civilian career, you used the GI Bill to earn an MBA and recently completed a doctorate in military history. Historical events have keenly interested you since you were a boy visiting the Greek battle site of Thermopylae. Learning how 300 Spartans fought to their death against thousands of Persians inspired you to pursue a military education. Your PhD specialty focuses on how weather can influence the outcome of military battles.

You are asked to speak at the National War College in Washington DC. Not to sell, but to speak as a guest historian. However, this lecture opportunity is great exposure for your company and its computer software that drives military weapon systems. You know that many influential Pentagon officials will attend. You are also excited and honored because it's your first opportunity to speak to a large group about your personal hobby and passion—history and how weather often decides military winners and losers.

Your allotted presentation time runs a very short 30 minutes. You plan 20 minutes to lay out your main theme and save 10 for an audience Q&A. You'll quickly summarize three historic battles in 15 minutes and use your last 5 to air your personal beliefs on adjusting military strategy to compensate for weather.

The first of the three campaigns you plan to cover is Napoleon's 1812 Russian invasion. The source for your information is a nineteenth-century graph by Charles J. Minard, a French civil engineer. His detailed study is often cited as an ideal statistical graph. Minard plotted six elements: troop strength, locations, dates, temperatures, distance, and the path to and retreat from Moscow. From this graph, you wish to pass on Minard's finding that the Cossacks didn't kill 412,000 Frenchmen—the chilling Russian spring rains, scorching summer heat, and freezing winter storms did.

As a visual, Minard's graph displays way too much information for viewers to digest in your limited presentation time (Figure 10.7). Besides, your interest is sharing Minard's conclusion, not touting his charting ability. Your focus is on the disaster, not the data.

Instead of Minard's graph, you show a portly Napoleon on horseback with many troops following. You talk about the Emperor entering Russia with a robust army of 422,000 soldiers. You relate the drenching, chilling, spring rains, the mud, the filth, then the heat, the flies, the dying, the long struggle toward Moscow, its disappointing battle, and finally the devastating retreat in the face of a freezing, winter blizzard. Your second slide shows a thinner Napoleon on a starving horse with a few crippled troops and a caption of 412,000 dead (Figure 10.8). You finish the French/Russian campaign relating how Napoleon recrosses the river where he started but now with only 10,000 troops. A horrendous defeat mainly driven by weather.

One might argue that some in the military audience would prefer Minard's original chart. For example, the chief pentagon

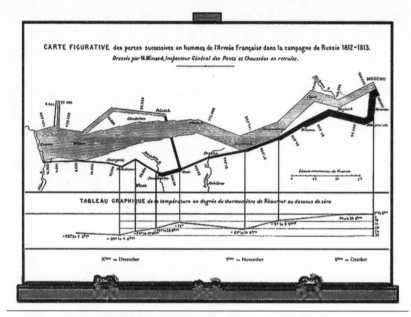

Figure 10.7 Napoleon's Russian Campaign

Figure 10.8 Napoleon's Retreat and Loss

meteorologist prefers seeing the range of Russian temperatures. An army general wants to compare the towns available to Napoleon to those used in Hitler's invasion. Or a senior pentagon statistician feels the audience needs to appreciate Minard's brilliant charting. All these are legitimate interests. But it's not their platform or their time to speak. Your presentation was to enlighten listeners on how weather effects military operations. Your goal was not to showcase or examine Minard's charting techniques.

Most presenters are under tight time constraints to make all their points. When only concluding information (an image visual) is shown, it's imperative that the presenter provide listeners with a detailed handout—in this example Minard's graph, the two image slides, and a text summary of your remarks. During your presentation, viewers assume your facts are correct and you are interpreting them fairly. (At least in this country, you are innocent until proven other wise—same with scientific research.) At the end, for verification, you provide a detailed handout that summarizes your content, assumptions, and conclusions.

When might you display Minard's detailed graph in a presentation? Suppose you were invited to speak to Naval Academy cadets on presenting statistical information. Four charts, like Minard's, with 15 minutes each would cover the ground nicely. With adequate time and 6 to 10 overlays, you could dramatize and point out the features of Minard's outstanding graph.

However, Minard's graph is not appropriate for this presentation. You selected three weather-driven campaigns and planned five short minutes of oral explanation and two image slides to support each of the three engagements. Then used two more slides for the concluding five minutes. Only image visuals can cover such a wide sweep and conclude so much data in such a short period. You're not losing time explaining Minard's six variables and having viewers wander independently through the information while you are drawing conclusions. You want each audience member's mind with you every step of the way. Too much information (most graphs and charts) is far more damaging to a presentation than too little information.

Your goal was straightforward. Paint a thumbnail sketch of the three campaigns and then share the disastrous results of each. From eight total slides, you want listeners to walk away convinced that weather should be a serious consideration in planning military campaigns. You need to keep the presentation simple, yet compelling, and backed with a few key numbers. One being that weather, not Russian troops, killed the majority of the 412,000 French soldiers.

For listeners, a few important numbers in a presentation are manageable. A multitude is not. Minard's graph alone contains well over a hundred data elements. Image visuals save huge amounts of time because they show the "forest" and eliminate viewers from wondering or getting lost among the "trees." Image visuals quickly portray exactly what listeners want—the overview, the findings, and the conclusion.

Think of the basic point of a presentation. Speakers gather information, analyze it, and present a conclusion or recommendations. This is true whether it's a sales pitch or a scientific study. The presenter does the homework for others. It doesn't mean speakers are always right or honest but simply that they "presented" their best efforts.

The validation comes later. Hence a detailed handout. If the validation had to come during the presentation, the pitch would take much longer. This would be very inefficient and few managers or senior executives would condone that.

Image slides, backed with a handout, are the perfect approach for delivering information, especially when the presentation time is short. Visual simplicity is a tough goal if you possess lots of information and expertise. Add to that mix selling to a large, diverse group and it's even harder. But shoot for simplicity using images.

11

Seeing the Range of Image Options: Seven Sample Presentations

"I like your motto. One picture is worth 1,000 denials."
—Ronald Reagan to the White House News
Photographers Association, May 18, 1983

The images you use are only limited by your imagination. When it comes to visuals, salespeople sometimes fall into predictable patterns: they display an image of the product, a chart illustrating rates of customer satisfaction, a photo of a satisfied customer, and so on. Their images are predictable, and predictable imagery does a poor job of selling. You want to use images to attract and focus attention, to provoke thought, to elicit emotion. This means that the images must not be boring or routine.

As you learned in the previous chapter, images must be tailored to a specific group and situation. This tailoring process, if done correctly, results in distinctive images. Because you're creating slides that are customized for a particular prospect's needs and concerns, they will naturally rise above the routine.

We've put together seven sample presentations to help you be aware of all the "colors in your palette." As you'll see, they represent an extremely wide range of possibilities. While we know that you probably won't find yourself in most of these situations, you will find yourself in different selling situations. From this chapter, you'll discover that you have more options for imagery than you might have considered.

Let's start out with a situation most of you have never been in: Selling the public on the FBI's preparedness for a terrorist attack.

Public Officials Speaking Out

Federal, state, or local government officials occasionally want to convince the public or media that they have made significant changes in policies, programs, or procedures. As a result, these officials hold press conferences where they attempt to communicate their points, often using large poster boards.

A typical example occurred May 29, 2002, when the FBI wished to improve its performance after the September 11 tragedy. The FBI called a press conference to announce how the Bureau would restructure its priorities. This was no small news release. The room was packed. The Attorney General accompanied the FBI Bureau Chief, who stood on the wrong side of a poster board covering key words (Figure 11.1).

Think about how you might employ this board, based on what you've learned about visual selling. Should the Attorney General or the Bureau Chief read the 10 points? Surely not. As we've pointed out earlier, salespeople should not just read bulleted points. Similarly, they also shouldn't ask their audience to read while they stand there twiddling their thumbs, since they are essentially ceding the visual focus to their bullet points.

In this instance, the Attorney General and the Bureau Chief chose to disregard the visual and dive directly into their prepared remarks. The problem: The TV audience and journalists probably didn't even listen until they read and absorbed the 10 points. The

Figure 11.1 FBI Photo

"in-their-face," overbearing, newsy visual was just too strong a draw. Because it simply sat there as back-up information, ignored by the speakers, it created an unhealthy competition between them and their visual.

What's the point of such an overwhelming text board? We know that some use these boards as a reminder of the main points they want to make, but index cards that only the speaker can see is a much more effective cuing device.

Let's assume the goal of the FBI was to say, "We are redefining priorities to better serve the United States." If that were correct, the bottom line for the FBI is to convey that the Bureau will become a stronger, more terror-responsive agency. The 10-point plan to achieve this is important but will be covered briefly and is not the bulk of the speech. In this case, the emphasis should be on its new strength, not the details. Images accomplish this by promoting the bigger picture. (No pun intended.) If the 10 points are to be covered quickly, here's an approach using a couple of poster boards.

The FBI Bureau Chief introduces the reshaped priorities by saying he'll (briefly or thoroughly) discuss the 10 points. He then states that the changes he's about to address will redirect a more focused Bureau.

He pauses as an aide positions a foam board on a tripod. The board has images that suggest the first five items, which the chief points to and identifies. Then an aide puts up a second board with five more images, and the director points to each and describes the priority. He or his aide then displays a final board with a large, FBI emblem at the center of the board. This colored image visually emphasizes the improvements. He ends by pointing to the emblem and adds that these ten reshaped priorities will strengthen and improve the Bureau, and he proceeds to the rest of his talk.

On the other hand, perhaps the chief plans to spend five minutes each on the 10 priority changes. In this case, he would create and display a single image of a board for the first priority, saying, "Of the 10 priorities, the first is to protect the United States from terrorist attacks." A color photo of a nondescript, high-rise, office building on fire is displayed (Figure 11.2). The

Figure 11.2 FBI Alternative 1

FBI chief continues with either a thorough or brief discussion of priority number 1.

The second priority, he says, is "to protect the United States against foreign intelligence operations and espionage." He pauses as he or an aide places on the tripod a board with an image of a terrorist, represented by a face hooded in a ski mask (Figure 11.3).

The Chief adds more details or moves to the third priority. The Chief covers the 10 points quickly or in detail.

After covering the 10 image points, the Chief takes questions or starts the next part of his speech. Addressing the ideas removes the news from the 10 points, so they don't sit there screaming for attention.

Only images, not text, allow the presenter and the visual to support each other and not compete one against the other. When you use images, you possess the flexibility to move through the information as quickly or thoroughly as needed. Also you're not

Figure 11.3 FBI Alternative 2

insulting viewers by reading to them. Only images lift a presentation out of the trench of details and up to a panoramic view.

Trial Lawyers Convincing Juries

Juries are similar to prospective customers listening to a detail-intensive pitch. They are hit with a great deal of information that you would like them to remember. If you've ever tried to sell a product or service based on data and detail, you understand the challenge lawyers face. How do you sway your prospects to your point of view without boring them to tears or overwhelming them with information? The answer is to incorporate visual elements. If retention is important, images are a superb tool for embedding ideas or swaying emotions. Exhibits in jury trials often are more memorable than anything a lawyer says. For instance, a lawyer continuously touches a stiff brace that the client must wear because of the defendant's negligence. Jury members vividly recall the constricting metal brace even months after the trial.

Let's look at a courtroom presentation that relied heavily on images to sell its argument to the jury. A freight delivery company, with a large fleet of trucks, suddenly hit the financial wall. The owners claimed their leased vehicles broke down too often and caused the company's bankruptcy. The freight company sued the leasing firm, charging that the poor-performing trucks ruined their business.

The defendant's attorney displayed image boards to accompany the opening remarks. His summarized words to the jury are below each visual.

"Were too many vehicles out of service? Let's first look at the overall locations of the trucks. The status of each truck, every day, is easy to determine. The driver had to fill in a trip ticket for every delivery" (Figure 11.4). "Collect a statistical sample of trip tickets and you'd know the location and activity of every truck, every day."

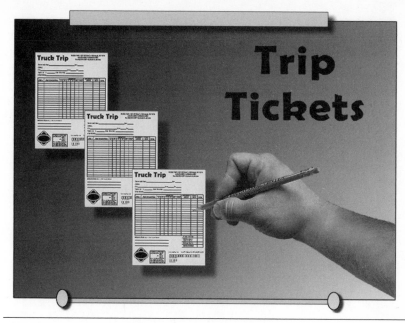

Figure 11.4 Trip Tickets

"The results of our sampling showed each truck could be categorized in one of three places: in the garage for repairs or sitting in the parking lot or making deliveries" (Figure 11.5).

"What did our statistical sample of trip tickets, for the last eight months, reveal? On an average day, 3 trucks were in the garage, 17 were out making deliveries, and 20 trucks were sitting in the parking lot. The problem, as you can see, and we'll prove, is that the 20 idled trucks mean that the XYZ Company just didn't have the business to support a fleet of 40 vehicles" (Figure 11.6).

"Now, what about the three trucks in the garage (Figure 11.7)? Is that good or bad performance? The records show only $1\frac{1}{3}$ trucks were repaired. The other $1\frac{2}{3}$ trucks were undergoing the manufacturer's scheduled maintenance. What about the $1\frac{1}{3}$ repair jobs? We'll show you that compared to industry standards, the $1\frac{1}{3}$ garaged vehicles, out of 40 trucks represents a very healthy fleet."

Figure 11.5 Truck Locations

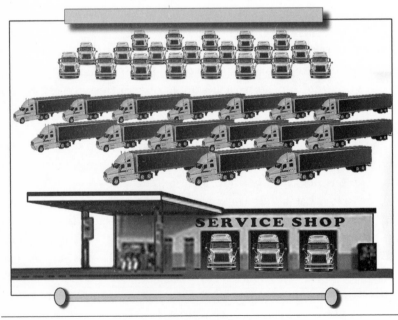

Figure 11.6 Idle Trucks

206

Figure 11.7 Garage Trucks

"Now, here's a question you might have been considering: What if we missed some trip tickets. Won't that throw off all these numbers? (Our client knew the other side would raise this issue.) Good thinking. We, of course, wanted to ensure all our numbers were accurate. Therefore, we crosschecked our statistical sample against the freight company's actual payroll (Figure 11.8).

"Our trip ticket sampling was highly correlated with employee payroll for those dates. In fact, it was nearly perfect. Therefore, we know that any missed trip tickets were insignificant."

The defense lawyer knew this case would be a fight over figures. He anticipated that his opponent would attempt to overwhelm the jury with details and numbers to distract them. Therefore, he wanted to end with a strong but humorous visual reminder that communicated they should take all his opponent's "number spewing" with a grain of salt (Figure 11.9).

As this attorney had anticipated, the plaintiff's lawyer used a sea of numbers, charts, and graphs. Thanks in large part to the

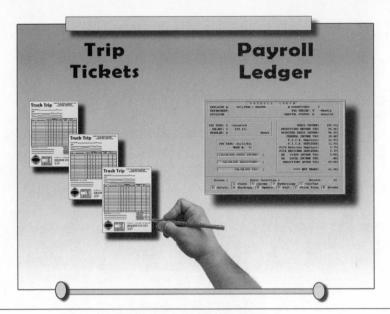

Figure 11.8 Payroll

Figure 11.9 Jury Box

defense attorney's astute visual approach, all the plaintiff's facts and figures had little impact on the jury, which then rendered the verdict of not guilty of all the charges.

Salespeople sometimes believe that facts and figures can make their cases. No doubt, you've sat in on sales presentations where a seemingly endless series of numbers and "factoids" were trotted out. No matter how impressive this raw data is, most prospective buyers quickly lose interest during a presentation. Perhaps there are ideal circumstances when a barrage of numbers is an effective selling tool—you have a technically inclined audience who quickly grasps and wants to hear all the specs. In most instances, however, people have little tolerance for "just the facts, just the numbers." They want them presented in an entertaining and memorable manner, and that means using images and displaying only key information.

Good lawyers also know that juries pay attention to images in a way they don't focus on raw data. In one recent case, senior executives were accused of deceiving shareholders as they looted the company's assets. The issue was whether the company was profitable, despite reported losses. Both sides presented financial records, but the plaintiff's attorneys recognized the need for a visual argument. As a result, they reduced the time spent presenting detailed numbers about the company's malfeasance and instead had a display of stacks in the courtroom of dollar bills and coins that suggested how much money was involved. These piles of money, stacked high on a table, drove home the plaintiff's point far more strongly than all the bar charts and income statements could do.

Evidence or legal arguments that turns into images often ensure intense recall. A photo taken of a brutal murder is a good example. Because a picture ignites such strong emotions, a photo of a severely mutilated child might not be shown to the jury. A judge could declare it too inflammatory or prejudicial. Still, many images are admissible, and they are not easily forgotten.

Besides boosting retention, images can communicate to the jury which pieces of evidence deserve special attention. In closing,

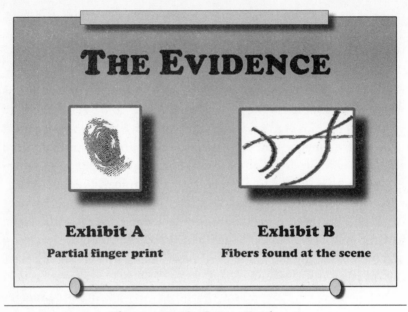

Figure 11.10 Crime Evidence

the attorney might use a prop or an image to spotlight the most important pieces of evidence or points, which the jury might otherwise undervalue. Enlarging physically small pieces of evidence heightens their credibility (Figure 11.10). These enlarged images are especially valuable in complex cases like patent infringement, embezzlement, or rate fixing.

Complex selling situations, therefore, cry out for visual elements. Recognize, too, that a competitor, like the defense attorney in an earlier example, may attempt to overwhelm a prospect with data. When you make a presentation that incorporates images, it will feel smooth, comprehensible, and clear by comparison.

Management Consultants Selling

Images can break the tie. When you're neck and neck with another competitor and you both are offering strong products and/or services, a good reputation, and similar pricing, images can be used to create an edge. This is especially true in the professional service firm arena. Law firms, ad agencies, accounting firms, consultancies, and other service firms often are similar to one another. Selection committees have difficulty isolating a specific attribute of one over another. The differentiator often comes down to a "feeling" that one firm will do a better job than the others, and this feeling often is a result of savvy presentation images.

Here's an example of how a professional service firm uses images to create the sense that they will be a superior service provider. Three high-powered consulting firms are competing for business at a car manufacturing company. The education and experience of the team members are critical. All three firms stress their consultants are both engineers and MBAs with just the right mix of technical and marketing expertise. Two of the competing firms show resume text slides like the one in Figure 11.11.

As this slide appears, the presenter reads what's already on the screen. Because the firm is using a deck, people are looking ahead to see the consultants' experience and schooling. The second firm employs this same approach.

Rachael Jackson, Design Engineer

- Formerly with Ford Thunderbird Design Team.
- BS and MA in Mechanical and Design Engineering, Purdue University, 1970
- MBA, University of Chicago, in Finance Technology
- Certified Mechanical Engineer,1980
- Ms. Jackson was usability lead for several design and redesign rounds of Ford high-end autos, including the original Thunderbird design in 1980.
- Her earlier affiliations include Belcore (Bell Communications Research) and General Motors.
- Ms. Jackson is on the editorial board of the publication <u>Mechanical Engineering Today</u> and the author of numerous articles...

Figure 11.11 Word Resume

It's the third firm that causes the prospective client to sit up and pay attention. When it comes to discussing the resumes, the first slide looks like Figure 11.12.

On the slide is a vehicle the potential client just happens to drive (a nice example of personalizing the slide) and a photo of one of the consultants examining a blueprint on the hood. The presenter points to Rachael in the slide and discusses her degrees. Then he points to the blueprint and relates her past relevant experience to the specific needs of the client. (A handout distributed *after* the presentation includes her detailed written resume.)

The next slide (Figure 11.13) shows another popular client car model with an illustration of Ryan, the second consultant, in a mechanic's uniform. The presenter points to Ryan and covers his education. Then, pointing to the toolbox, the presenter explains Ryan's pertinent past consulting jobs.

Figure 11.12 Rachael Image Resume

Figure 11.13 Ryan Image Resume

These two images are more eye-catching, personalized, and creative than any text slide could ever be. They communicate all sorts of intangibles about the consulting firm and stick in people's minds. They bring Ryan and Rachael to life for the prospective client; they are differentiated from the other consultants in similarly nice outfits and given distinct, attractive qualities. It's not that the other firms lack people like Ryan and Rachael. It's simply that they just talked about them rather than animated them using images.

Financial Consultants Building Relationships

Seminars have become common selling tools for everyone from investment firms to vacation time share packagers. You may have no interest in seminar selling, but you are interested in forming strong relationships with prospects and customers. As we'll see, images are critical to laying the foundation of these relationships.

Start out by imagining you're holding a financial seminar, and you send announcements through the mail. The invitation promises people will learn how to diversify their portfolio, maximize their assets for retirement, or ensure they don't outlive their savings. They are worried about saving money for their child's education or they are approaching retirement age, so they decide to invest the two hours the seminar requires. The seminar invitation also mentions a free meal or complimentary hors d'oeuvres.

As people drive to the seminar, they think about what ideally could happen. Of course, they hope to learn something about investing. But foremost, they would love to meet an advisor who has the ability to grow portfolios, not just generate fees or commissions. And last, they wish for an interesting evening—not a boring, talking head. They see enough of those presentations at work.

As the room darkens and the first twisting, spaghetti-line graph wiggles across the screen, accompanied by a lengthy technical explanation, they sink down in their chairs (Figure 11.14).

When the third visual appears, another boring bar chart, they know they've been had. It's going to be a long, dull time until the free "eats." By the fifth visual, a wordy text slide, a few brave souls consider visiting the washroom, then sneaking out to their cars.

No matter what type of seminar selling you're involved in, you're really selling a relationship. You're asking a prospective customer to trust you, even though he or she doesn't know you. You're trying to communicate that you're honest, knowledgeable, and able to help him or her deal with tough, complex issues. That is asking a lot. It's very difficult to establish a relationship with a prospective seminar customer in a visually cold environment. Think about what happened in our example.

First, in a dark room, all the emphasis is on the screen. Is the speaker peddling information or trying to establish the beginnings of a relationship? If it's the relationship, people need to see the presenter. Investors look for an advisor who conveys expertise

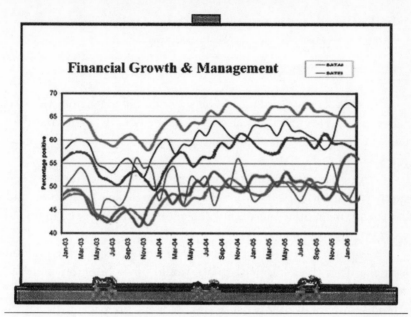

Figure 11.14 Spaghetti Chart

and trustworthiness. The facts alone, as impressive as they might be, don't communicate these traits. At best, they may be interesting and thought provoking. But you don't hand over your portfolio to someone who is merely interesting and thought provoking. You need the beginning of a relationship to make a buying decision in a seminar, and if you're literally and figurative left in the dark (even if the expensive graphs show up well on the screen), you're not going to make that decision. Darkness hides negative traits and makes people suspicious. Positive traits shine in a well-lit room.

The introductory slides say little about the seminar presenter. There is no sense of his or her personality or financial management philosophy. No dynamic interplay exists between what the seminar leader says and what the slides show. He or she doesn't use any of the problems that are on their mind to start creating a relationship. For instance, here are three issues seminar attendees are concerned about:

1. Too much conflicting investing advice
2. Whom to trust to manage their money
3. The five biggest investing mistakes they can make

Let's take the third idea. The seller quickly mentions the five mistakes, and then says, "Let me fill in the details of the first faux pas—jumping on investment ideas gleaned from the popular press" (Figure 11.15).

An outstanding seminar presenter walks a fine line between supplying information and entertainment. The free food and drinks are nice, but they are not the entertainment or the main attraction. The speaker is.

Obviously, a presentation needs substance. But content alone isn't the draw. If it were, attendees would buy a book on their favorite financial topic and stay home for a comfortable read. People attend seminars in part because they're lazy. They want the infor-

Figure 11.15 The Financial Press

mation spoon fed to them and they want it to go down easy. When they see the first five mistakes slide, they appreciate its humor. When they see the second one, they relish the distinct point of view it conveys. Together, the slides tell attendees that the seminar presenter has the attractive quality of being humorous, and that he or she also has developed a strong perspective on mistakes investors make. This humanizes him or her and nudges the group toward the start of a relationship.

For seminar sellers, success means having attendees call them for a follow-up visit. Certainly, sellers have to motivate people with their ideas and information, but they also have to forge a relationship in the seminar. People won't call a seminar leader without that sense of connection. Because sellers present to a number of people in a short period, they can't connect one on one. While the images presenters use aren't going to create a complete bond, they can help lay the groundwork for this relationship. The goal is to get people to call for that all-important appointment and that's when the seminar presenter can switch to one-on-one selling that results in a true relationship. The images, though, create an interpersonal environment that promotes that opportunity.

Entrepreneurs Raising Money

At some point in your career, you may need to convince someone to make a sizeable investment in you in money or personal backing. The example we're going to use is an entrepreneur trying to raise funds from venture capitalists. The principle, though, applies whether you're trying to get your boss to back your idea or you are trying to raise money for a good cause. In all these instances, people fail to attract support for two reasons: They lose focus or fail to simplify the complex. As you'll discover, images can help you avoid these mistakes.

A venture capitalist drools at the thought of underwriting the next Google, Amazon, or E-Bay. Therefore, they sponsor yearly conferences in major cities for start-up companies to present their business ideas. For efficiency, venture capitalists limit the speaking time and even suggest content structures that keep presenters on track and potential investors awake.

Entrepreneurs commit the mistake of losing focus in these situations because they don't realize the real objective of these conferences. They act as if they can simply present their idea without focusing on selling competitively. In other words, they sell as if they aren't competing with any other entrepreneurs for venture capital money. From a selling standpoint, their presentation is unfocused. It doesn't suggest why they, out of all the entrepreneurs asking for funding, should be selected. As the saying goes, many are called but only a few are chosen. Only a small number of start-ups ever interest investors enough to fund them.

Unfocused entrepreneurs project text slides on a distant screen that always turns into an impersonal, split presentation. The time is limited. The structure is fixed. These entrepreneurs present as if they lack the freedom to be creative or unique in their approach.

For example, venture capitalists usually ask founders to cover their qualifications. Typically, entrepreneurs spend too much time listing all their degrees and accomplishments. Given that time is limited, a significant portion of the presentation isn't focused on selling. Venture capitalists invest based on sound business plans and great ideas, not on whether someone has an MBA or went to Harvard or worked at a Fortune 100 company. Nonetheless, entrepreneurs show their qualifications as long, wordy text slides (Figure 11.16).

A focused seller, on the other hand, will flash the credentials quickly on the screen and provide venture capitalists with a more detailed resume later. They won't waste precious time and visual space on a long list of credentials that can't even be fully read and is quickly forgotten.

A much better visual approach is to present credentials via an image. Let's say a team of scientists has a potential cure for cancer and needs $5 million for their start-up company. They might project the image slide shown in Figure 11.17.

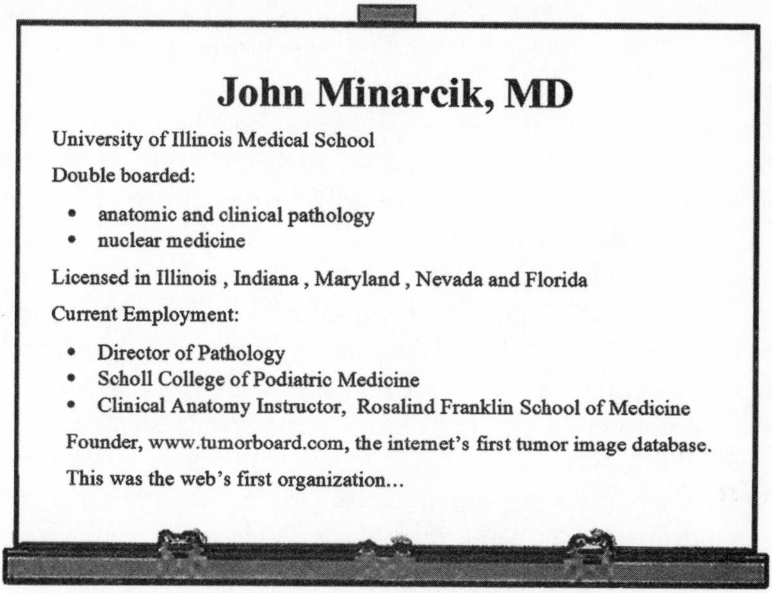

John Minarcik, MD

University of Illinois Medical School

Double boarded:

- anatomic and clinical pathology
- nuclear medicine

Licensed in Illinois , Indiana , Maryland , Nevada and Florida

Current Employment:

- Director of Pathology
- Scholl College of Podiatric Medicine
- Clinical Anatomy Instructor, Rosalind Franklin School of Medicine

Founder, www.tumorboard.com, the internet's first tumor image database.

This was the web's first organization...

Figure 11.16 VC Word Resume

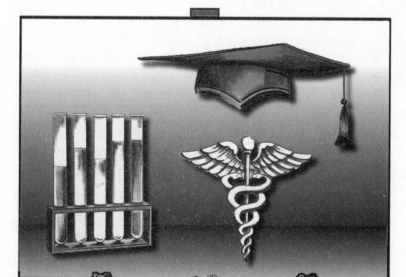

Figure 11.17 VC Image Resume

Then, the CEO scientist might say, "We're three MDs (points to the staff insignia), and PhDs in biochemistry (points to the test tube rack) with positions as medical school researchers (points to the mortar board cap). Please come by our booth this afternoon. We'll check your pulses and hand you our business packet, including our resumes showing our extensive and expensive educations. Our parents are still swimming in debt! Now, on to our medical breakthrough."

The second mistake is failing to simplify. Start-up founders are often PhDs, MDs, or MBAs, presenting sophisticated, technical innovations. They forget that they are talking to nontechnical investors. Recall that most doctors, when speaking with patients, use everyday language, not big words or Latin terms. Doctors use the same simple explanations for either the high school dropout or the college graduate. A physician won't shift to a medical school vocabulary just because the patient earned a university degree. In fact, doctors do the opposite (or at least they should), so that all patients clearly understand the diagnosis or treatment recommendations.

Let's say a pharmaceutical start-up discovers a new coating for oral medications. This special glaze has built-in, controllable absorption features. The medicine in pills can now be forced much faster into the bloodstream or released very slowly.

A PhD, MD presenter projects Figure 11.18 and says: "You'll see how the induced palliation agent reacts to the epidermis receptor and causes enzyme permeability to cumulate."

It's unlikely that anyone in the crowd will get "permeability cumulation" or any of the technical terms used. To explain to nonmedical listeners how the coating works, the presenter might start with a simple analogy driven by images. For example, he or she introduces the explanation by discussing how some foods are absorbed quickly and others slowly (Figures 11.19 and 11.20).

"As you might know, a martini shoots into the bloodstream . . .

"On the other hand, a steak sits heavily in your stomach before it's broken down, digested, and enters the bloodstream . . ."

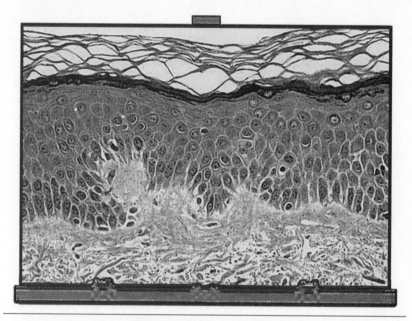

Figure 11.18 Cell Slide

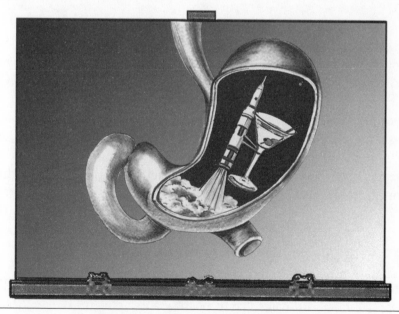

Figure 11.19 Martini in Stomach

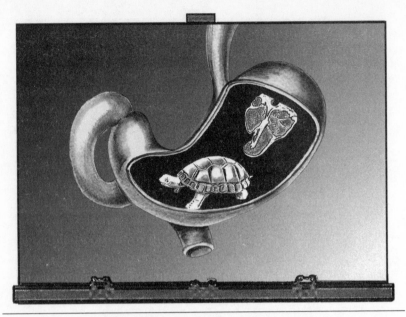

Figure 11.20 Steak in Stomach

"With our new coatings, we can delivery a pill that acts like a cocktail, a steak, or anything in between, depending on the desired absorption rate." For venture capital presentations, image visuals convey complex ideas quickly and simply. The last thing entrepreneurs want is for a venture capitalist to struggle with a product concept. In the initial presentations, you don't have to explain every technical detail. Instead, you have to capture the "funder's" imagination. A simple but ingenious concept, conveyed with maximum speed and impact through just the right image, does exactly that.

Corporate Executives Persuading

If you work for an organization of any size, you are constantly selling your subordinates, your bosses, and your team members. Sometimes, this selling is informal: "Can you please make sure you get this report done by tomorrow?" Other times, though, you must engage in a more formal selling presentation. It may involve motivating your staff to work harder and longer than they have in the past. It may be focused on getting the company's senior staff to approve a new initiative. Whatever it is that you're selling in these organizational situations, images can play a huge role in your success.

If you're the CEO, you may not need as much help to sell people on something as others in the company; people tend to buy what a CEO has to say because of his or her stature. Most other corporate types, though, have a tougher time of it. If you've ever sat through a human resources presentation and listened to an HR manager try to convince people to adopt a policy they aren't interested in or don't believe in, you know that this is a big selling challenge.

Nonetheless, you can increase your odds of selling successfully to this internal customer if you entertain as well as inform. Unfortunately, most executives don't do a particular good job of achieving either goal. Instead, they plaster the screen with text slides that look like Figure 11.21.

Now compare the this information to the equivalent image slide in Figure 11.22 and the speaker's opening lines.

"Let me move into how management specifically proposes to cut cost, which puts the savings into your pension plan."

"First, by cutting consultants we'll put the operational decisions back in your hands where it belongs (Figure 11.23). You are the backbone of this company, not the consultants."

"If the phones in our numerous call centers aren't ringing more than 80 percent of the time, management plans to close that center to save money" (Figure 11.24).

"Maybe we should make those marketing folks ride on the tail; then they won't be flying to so many palm tree destinations (Figure 11.25). No seriously, business travel has become a real drag on profitability."

Image presentations offer the opportunity to liven up what can be dull subjects. They allow you to sell with humor, to use visuals

Achieving Hiccup Inc.'s Corporate Goals and Cutting Unnecessary Costs:

- Reduce the overuse of consultants
- Eliminate unprofitable call centers
- Tightly control business trips

Figure 11.21 Bullet Point List

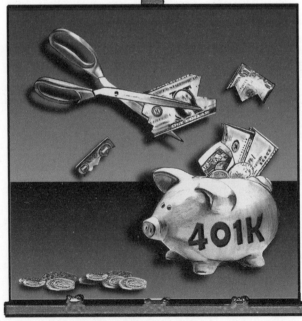

Figure 11.22 401(k)

Figure 11.23 Eliminate Consultants

Figure 11.24 Call Centers

Figure 11.25 Cut Air Travel

that resonate with people in your company, and to be provocative and informative simultaneously. You know your audience better than you know most outside prospects, and so you can create images that are particularly on the mark. Use this knowledge to your advantage the next time you make an internal presentation.

Scientists Selling a Complex Concept

Some selling situations involve much greater complexity than others do. It is one thing to sell a pair of shoes or any item where the prospective buyer immediately understands the product or service. It's something else to sell a product or service where the prospect has only a vague sense of how it works. In these latter situations, visual selling offers a distinct advantage over purely verbal selling. Images can clarify the complex much faster than spoken words.

When time and the attention span of prospects are limited, visual selling communicates even difficult scientific concepts with speed and impact.

Before 1996, simple blood tests to diagnose disease were performed one at a time in a single tube, which was a slow and laborious task. At that time, start-up company Luminex Inc. created a prototype of a computerized, countertop device that could perform hundreds of blood tests simultaneously in the same tube in less than 15 minutes.

Luminex was founded by a high-powered team—Drs. Mark Chandler, Ralph McDade, and Mike Spain. These men were long on business savvy, likeability, and intelligence (two PhDs in immunology and biochemistry and an MD). When they started to market their device to pharmaceutical firms and Wall Street, however, they hit heavy sales resistance. Their prototype blood analyzer operated with laser beams, colored beads, multiple dyes, and computer software. It was not easy to explain a sophisticated laser combined with a complex chemical system to potential clients, investors, or the FDA. They knew they had designed and built an innovative, much-needed device, but they also knew they weren't getting their message across.

Eventually they switched from an exclusively verbal to a more visual selling approach. The three founders changed their delivery techniques. They revamped their sales strategy in many visual ways, including changing their PowerPoint presentations to emphasize images, not words.

Dr. Ralph McDade, one of the founders and chief scientist, hit the sales circuit with the new, visual presentation, talking again to corporate investors, the FDA, scientific meetings, and large organizations. Using this different approach, he discovered he no longer was staring out at blank, uncomprehending faces. The nods and smiles demonstrated that he was getting through to them. As he walked out of an important initial sales presentation to top management at a major pharmaceutical firm, one senior vice president said to him, "If your instrument is half as good as your presentation, you have a phenomenal device."

In the company's first year, Dr. McDade delivered some 200 presentations. At one scientific conference in Japan, Ralph spoke toward the end of a long day. As he waited his turn, he saw that the attention of many in the large audience was wandering, and some were dozing. Then he stood up to present. As his initial images hit the screen, he saw heads rise and eyes all across the ballroom focus on him. He had his audience again in the palm of his hand, even across language and culture.

The founders identified another opportunity a number of years later after Luminex had achieved success. With the ability to perform hundreds of blood tests quickly and efficiently, scientists could now tell a great deal about the general health and well-being of the human body. Biomarkers, chemicals in the blood, can indicate whether an individual has entered the earliest stages of a disease when the proper therapies are the most effective. Drs. Chandler, McDade, and Spain launched Biophysical Inc. to sell these tests to consumers.

Selling to consumers was different from selling to key corporate accounts or Wall Street, but they trusted in the same visual approach and adapted it to the consumer market. Again, they created new sales and scientific presentations using images. And again, they got off to a fast, successful start.

Figures 11.26 through 11.29 are samples from one presentation to illustrate their use of visual selling.

"Biomarkers are blood-based chemicals whose levels are altered by disease or other medical conditions. With just a few drops of blood, biomarker patterns can be identified that allow disease to be detected early when treatment options are most effective" (Figure 11.26).

"The beads represent 250 biomarker tests of your blood. Our experts interpret those test results to give you a comprehensive profile of your personal well-being and health risk factors" (Figure 11.27).

"Most of us view the night sky as a beautiful collection of stars. Few however, have the ability to see and point out the many constellations. Biomarker patterns are very much like the constellations. It's prudent to understand them and then make lifestyle changes and take whatever preventive medical actions you can" (Figure 11.28).

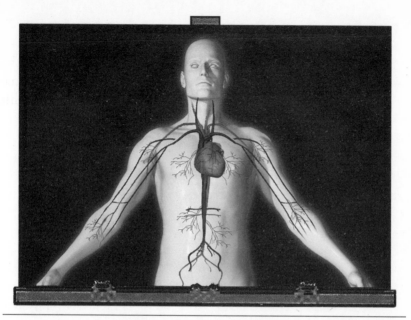

Figure 11.26 Vein Man

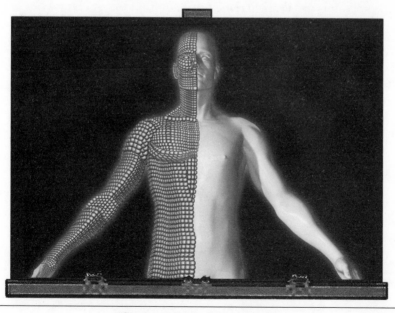

Figure 11.27 Biomarkers

Figure 11.28 The Night Sky

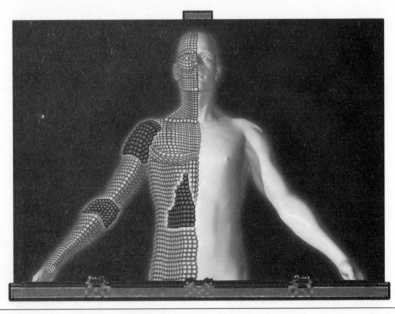

Figure 11.29 Bead Man

"Our Biophysical MDs, who specialize in the study of bio-markers, personalize a test that can detect the early stages of can-cer, cardiovascular disease, diabetes, and numerous other medical conditions . . ." (Figure 11.29).

(Biophysical's consumer and scientific presentation contain still images, fades from one image into another and video clips. These four images are, of course, static. In the actual slide pre-sentation, for example, the beads in Figure 11.27 dissolve into the stars of the night sky where moving lines outline the three constellations.)

Keep Your Options Open

We've thrown a lot of images at you, but we've done so with a pur-pose. We want you to be aware that you have multiple visual alter-natives—some good, some bad, some indifferent. Don't limit yourself to one particular visual approach—it may be that you have to shift visual styles as you change from one selling situation to the next. Consider all the potential visuals you have at your dis-posal—charts, graphs, pictograms, photos, illustrations, cartoons, and montages. The list of possibilities goes on and on. Treat these possibilities as a menu to select from.

Your advantage is that you are now aware of what works and what doesn't. You are more educated about visual selling than your peers and competitors. Use this knowledge—and all the options open to you—to craft a highly effective visual pitch. And see if you don't "win" more often.

CHAPTER

12

How to Sell Doctors on Washing Their Hands and Other Final Insights

"If a man empties his purse into his head, no one can take it away from him. An investment in knowledge always pays the best interest."

—Benjamin Franklin

The best news we can give you is that it's easier to create an effective sales presentation today than ever before. While more competition may exist for each prospect, the competition isn't particularly adept at selling. So many salespeople rely on a standard, text/screen pitch that, in many instances, all it takes to win is a presentation with visual dash.

Today, few sell. Most simply run out a "show and tell." More accurately, they just tell.

In the distant past, selling required mastering the art of persuasion, relying on both speaking ability and physical delivery skills. Ideas were unfolded with burning enthusiasm, sincerity, and rarely read from a script. Consequently, thousands of salespeople learned the logic that would overcome objections and nudge prospects toward "yes." Then came the shortcuts.

The overhead projector allowed people to skip memorizing content and lean on projected crib notes. The ubiquitous 35 mm slide-projector soon legitimized this laziness and allowed even bankers, lawyers, and accountants who had never sold anything in their lives to think they were selling.

Salespeople no longer had to face prospects. They could darken the room, hide in the back, and flood the screen with their pitch. The end of effective selling was near. The screen became the center of attention and the sellers stood behind a "curtain."

PowerPoint delivered the deathblow. Today, everybody thinks they're selling when all they're really doing is spelling—getting the words on the slides right. People read the slides verbatim or close to it, and the salesperson relies completely on a lifeless presentation. Most don't capitalize on their own presence or the potential power of other images.

Just prior to the 1929 crash, John D. Rockefeller pulled out of the stock market after a shoeshine boy offered him several hot tips. He figured, rightly, that if all of Wall Street right down to the boot polishers were "buying," it was time to sell. The same scenario is now true of the millions depending on their laptop or room screen to deliver the sale. Bailing out is long overdue.

For 25 years, we've attempted to convince clients to sell, not tell; to put the focus back on the messenger; to reposition salespeople so they can do what they do best—motivate people to buy.

Throughout this book, we've also tried to provide you with the rationale and tools to achieve these goals. You've learned that sellers, not screens must deliver the message; that delivery skills must be persuasive since prospects should look largely at you; that visuals must be designed so they don't dominate or compete with the seller; that the room set-up has to channel attention toward the seller, not the screen or laptop.

If you want to be a master visual seller, you need to keep one word in mind—control. Unless you are maximizing all that is in your control, you're simply telling, not selling. A well-known Pirelli tire ad shows the importance of control in a visual way. It pictures Carl Lewis, the famous Olympic sprinter, in a starting position and wearing red high-heel shoes (Figure 12.1). Lewis would have no control if he bolted up and tried to race down the track. The words at the top of the ad say, "Power is nothing without control." The same holds for selling an idea, product, or service.

You need to do more than throw in some graphics to your presentation or make sure to use gestures when you speak. Instead, you must control the visual elements of your presentation. You must think through all the visual aspects we've discussed and then tailor your visual approach to your audience and to the message you want to deliver. After considering all your visual options, you should implement the ones that will create the maximum impact. By taking these actions, you control what is seen rather than be controlled by it.

Figure 12.1 Power Is Nothing without Control

At this point, we hope that most of you are sold on these visual selling concepts, but we also suspect that at least some of you are overwhelmed at the prospect of putting them into practice. No question, we've given you a lot to think about and to do. At the same time, recognize that you don't have to do everything all at once. We encourage you to start small. Specifically, here is a five-step program to get you started:

1. Assess your visual selling performance by asking the following questions:
   —Do you ever consider the visual aspects before, during, or after a sales presentation?
   —Do you pay attention to one visual aspect (i.e., your clothes) but ignore the others?
   —Do you consider visual elements but are too lazy or lack the knowledge to change your pitch in order to sell more visually?
   —Do you attempt to create more compelling visuals or make sure all eyes are focused on you, but that you don't do a very good job?
   —Do you find that you're able to create a strong visual presentation in one area but not in another?
   —Do you try to rehearse not only your verbal presentation but also your visual one?
   —Do you solicit feedback from colleagues or prospective customers about all aspects of your presentation, including visual elements?
   —Do you make an effort to change your visual approach to suit your message and your viewers?
2. Based on your assessment, target one visual element or skill to improve. Perhaps you decide you're going to focus on making better eye contact with prospects. Perhaps you want to start replacing a text slide or two with more meaningful images. Whatever your choice, concentrate on making this

small improvement when you make your next presentation. Be sure to rehearse whatever this visual improvement entails prior to the actual presentation.

3. Once you've mastered a given skill or element, add another one to the mix. For instance, now that you've done a good job making eye contact with the group, incorporate gestures to underline important points. When you add the second element, however, make sure you don't forget about the first one. Both should now be part of your selling approach.

4. Add one element at a time, similar to the previous step. Make sure you don't bite off more than you can handle. If you start feeling overwhelmed, stop adding visual elements to your sales presentation and stick with what works for you. The goal, though, is to reach a comfort level with one skill or element and then add another until your visual selling engine is firing on all cylinders.

5. Ask a colleague or friend to review your visually enhanced selling method, either in rehearsal or at a specific presentation. Choose someone who you know will offer you honest feedback. Ask them about the various visual elements you've incorporated. Did your images create a memorable, convincing message? Were your gestures well timed and smooth? Did you use a prop effectively? Was your attire appropriate for the selling situation? Did you create a visually friendly room set-up? Did you maintain the group's focus or did their attention wander to a screen or elsewhere? Make adjustments based on this feedback.

Finally, we'd like to leave you with a story from the book, *Freakonomics*, by Stephen J. Dubner and Steven D. Levitt. They explain that at Los Angeles' Cedars-Sinai Medical Center, the hospital administration was concerned that a relatively low percentage of doctors practiced good hand-washing hygiene. It was theorized that this lack of hand washing helped pass on bacterial infections to patients. As a result, the hospital attempted to motivate doctors to wash their hands regularly, doing everything from bombarding doctors with e-mails and faxes urging them to wash their hands to offering Starbucks gift certificates as incentives to do so. While they moved the compliance rate higher than it was, it still fell far short of their goal of 100 percent compliance.

Then, during a meeting of top doctors, the hospital's epidemiologist gave the doctors agar plates (a sterile Petri dish) and asked them to press their hands into the plates. The epidemiologist sent the plates to a lab, and they were cultured and photographed. The photos were shocking and eye-catching, though not in a pleasant way. They showed huge colonies of bacteria, and no doubt anyone looking at them could imagine how they might infect anyone who came to close to them. The administration then took these photographs and turned them into screen savers that popped up on every computer in the hospital. Shortly thereafter, hand-washing compliance rose close to 100 percent.

We relate this story to emphasize the power of images to persuade. No matter how much the hospital administration talked to doctors about the need for hand washing, a significant percentage of doctors refused to buy the argument. It was only when they were shown a striking image that they changed their minds and bought the argument the administration was making.

We realize that while visual selling is a paradigm shift, it isn't a panacea. You can't expect that choosing the right image will automatically turn a disinterested prospect into a buyer. What you can expect, however, is an increased focus on visual elements will make a difference in your selling effectiveness. In a world where many sellers remain blind to visual tools and dedicated to PowerPoint text slides, it can provide you with a significant competitive edge.

Afterword

If you would like to know about our course materials, seminars, and consulting, visit www.visualselling.biz.

We specialize in rehearsing executives for high-stakes competitive presentations, outside funding pitches, and large audience addresses.

The Team: Peg Corwin, Paul LeRoux, and Constance Trojnar

References

Canadian Cancer Society. 2000. Larger cigarette warnings with photos of health effects would be effective at discouraging smoking, concludes Canadian Cancer Society Research. Media release, January 18. Non-Smokers Rights Association. www.nsra-adnf.ca

Higbee, Kenneth L. 2001. *Your memory: How it works and how to improve it*. 2nd ed. New York: Marlowe and Company.

Messaris, Paul. 1997. *Visual persuasion: The role of images in advertising*. Thousand Oaks, CA: Sage Publications.

Miller, George A. 1956. The magic number seven, plus or minus two: Some limits for processing information. *Psychology Review* 63 (2), 81–97.

Oldash, Mark. 2000. *Creativity for graphic designers*. Cincinnati, OH: North Light Books.

Rindsberg, Steve. "What resolution should I make my images for PowerPoint slide shows." http://office.microsoft.com/en-us/powerpoint/HA011163551033.aspx

Shepard, R. N. 1967. Recognition memory for words, sentences and pictures. *Journal of Verbal Learning and Verbal Behavior* 6, 156–63.

Sinatra, Richard. 1986. *Visual literacy connections to thinking, reading, and writing*. Springfield, IL: Charles C Thomas.

Index

A

Action words, using, 24–25
Adrenaline surge, results of, 18–19
Advantages, selling, using images, 153–154
Agenda slide, 157
Anxiety, handling, 18–28
Aristotle, 3
Art boards, 182
Artists, working with, 152–153
Attention:
    holding, 17–39
    managing, 10–11
Auditory messages, visual and, 13–14

B

Benefits:
    building, 163–165
    definition of, 163
    tailoring images to match, 165

Bonaparte, Napoleon, 34
Booth design, 180–181
Buyers, what they are looking at, 3–15

C

Canadian cigarettes, 5–7
Chanel, Coco, 173
Charisma, 99–100
Chunking, 90
Clothes, choosing what to wear, 36–39
Comfort, clothes and, 39
Comments, questions versus, 48–49
Competitive presentations, 174
Compliments, for the questioner, 49–50
Concepts, finding, 105–106
Conservative versus aggressive images, 113–116
Consulting and courses, 239